The Whispering

GOD

By
Jeanene Hanna Wagner & Paul A. Wagner, Ph.D.

3rd Coast Books, LLC
19790 Hwy. 105 W. Ste. 1318
Montgomery, Texas 77356

3rd Coast Books, LLC
19790 Hwy. 105 W. Ste. 1318
Montgomery, TX 77356

www.3rd CoastBooks.com

ISBNs
Perfect Binding (Print) 978-1-946743-63-3
eBook/Mobi 978-1-946743-64-0
eBook/ePub 978-1-946743-65-7

Publisher-Ron W. Mumford
Project Coordinator - Ian W. Gorman, MBA, Co-Publisher
Editors - Ian W. Gorman MBA, Faye Walker, Ph.D.
Cover Artist - Kathleen J. Shields, Kathleen's Graphics
Text Designer - Kathleen J. Shields, Kathleen's Graphics
Video Trailer - Alex Gonzales
Marketing/PR - Pamela K. Ott, Kay Pinkerton, M.A., PR

Library of Congress Control Number: 2022919393

Dedication

We dedicate this book to our parents, each of whom has passed. We also dedicate this book to our children and all family members in the hope that one day they, and other readers, may find grounds to listen further to the feel of the whispering God. We also dedicate this book to our friends and other family who have passed on. There are too many to list, and the number grows exponentially as we age. In addition, those who have passed on to the afterworld are settled in. This book is for those here on earth who have yet to finish their journey toward destiny.

Table of Contents

Acknowledgments

There are too many people to list. We have been fortunate to have many tutors along the way. Indeed, every faithful Christian we have met is someone to whom we each owe an acknowledgment. And to each lost soul who has shared their personal befuddlement, we have learned from them as well. Having said this, we would be remiss not to mention three personal friends who are also pastors who have been especially present in our lives together: Dr. Ed Young, Reverend Gary Thomas, and Rabbi Jason Sobel.

And there have been many authors of the recent past whose writings tutored us as well. Writers such as C.S. Lewis, Thomas V. Morris, Peter Kreeft, Richard Foster, and, most especially, the philosopher William P. Alston. Alston convincingly explains that it is through experience that people become mindful of the divine. Experience brings us to the Great Path of God's plan for all. The study of scripture fills in the blanks and helps keep believers focused on the path revealed through experiential enlightenment.

Preface

In this monograph, two ordinary persons share their insights and combine over one hundred and thirty years of experience. One has experience in the academic and corporate world, and the other has experience in the world of Hollywood entertainment, Country and Western music, and thoroughbred racing. There has been much bewilderment about religious matters for each of us over the years. And, happy to say, there has been modest success for each of us aligning our plans with **The Plan** Jesus reported God having for all.

The Plan Jesus spoke of is addressed to all believers. It is not a confining imposition on a few, a benefaction for others, nor an option for only select believers. **The Plan** is open to believers of independent free will. It is a broad path with much room to wander and yet remain on the planned path for all. For those who contrive the phrase "…a plan for you…." as if it is directed to this or that person rather than to all believers, such a reading threatens understanding **God's Great Gift. God's Great Gift** is to make us in His image. This does not mean all embodied persons look alike. And science has shown that in the one percent of genetic mapping that separates one person from another, there is great apparent diversity. Persons are in God's image because of free will.

Neuroscientists have shown that free will is more limited than many unfamiliar with science believe. However, Alfred Mele and others have shown that persons have autonomy. Autonomy here, as taken from Immanuel Kant's thinking of more than a century ago, is the *ability to override a potentially bad decision*.

Think about the gravity of this ability. The story of Jonah, the story of Lot's wife both show the failure of resisting the temptation of a bad idea. Even the parable of the rich man insufficiently in control of his life testifies to the importance of treasuring the capacity of free will to override the power of bad ideas.

The great Augustine in his *Confessions* illuminates the profoundness of neglecting this ability. The capacity that privileges persons as reflections of the image of God can be developed into an ability for overriding bad decisions. For example, it is neglect of this developing ability that Augustine writes about when describing his great sin.

Augustine's great sin was destroying apples in an orchard. He did not steal the apples. He did not eat them. He simply destroyed them. Sheer want and nothing more was driving his body and his behavior. No thought was given to **God's Great Plan**. No thought was given to anything other than Augustine's want to destroy.

Augustine exercised no autonomy. He simply surrendered to brute wants of the moment, a bad idea. In **God's Plan**, as Augustine, Aquinas, and even James the apostle each indicate, following **God's Plan** is a decision we make to do something other than satisfying brute wants of mind, heart, or body. In other words, we are responsible for what we do. We are responsible for navigating the **Great Planned Path of God**, but we are just as free to leave it – such is the nature of free will. For example, James writes that faith in the absence of good works is dead. Agents of free will are responsible for chosen indiscretions.

As part of **God's Great Gift** of free will, there is also **The Great Promise. The Great Promise** is God's pledge never to abandon us. In contrast, persons can abandon God. Yet even in the face of will-fully bad decision-making, God pledges never to abandon persons. Persons here refers to hominids that are embodied, that is to say, those who are soul-ful. At present, all hominids are persons. That is to say, all now are embodied persons. They have souls.

When the journey of life is finished, persons will have either abandoned or communed with the will of God. Any division between God and person will be eternal, as will any final commitment to commune with God. Until then, **The Great Promise** never to abandon people behaving well or badly is sacrosanct. Yet never forget: the gift of human free will has a tax associated with it. The very people God loves and privileges can act on a bad idea: namely, to abandon God. And some do.

The purpose of this small book is to give readers the moment each may need to meditate and discern good ideas from those that are, as Augustine frankly admits, bad. There is no philosophy of good or bad in the pages that follow. Just as Augustine does not record in his *Confessions*, he does not elaborate on the orchard offense to God. When service to God or others is set aside just to surrender to pointless temptation to do wrong, no philosophy is needed.

In contemporary lingo, this book is for you to use to pump the brakes in your life. Slow down. Think about your mindful anticipations. Make decisions as you are free to do with God in mind. A moment to think WWJD never destroyed anyone's life or chance at happiness.

We use the seasons of the year as a metaphorical model prompting particular attention to some especially likely moments needing meditative attention. The book offers no answers. Through meditation, it has been our experience, individually and collectively, that in the silence, God whispers the answers needed. No booming voice. No spreading apart of the heavens. An audience with God is always available for one who meditates. By meditation here, we mean prayer wherein one subordinates his or her wants and anxieties and instead focuses on staying open to the feel of God's whispers in response.

The choice on analogizing the journey of life by comparison with the seasons of a year has, too, the advantage of illuminating the need for flexibility of imagination. Any season's length may vary somewhat from year to year and from geographic context to geographic context in historic time. So it is with each human life. And while both the set of four seasons and the length of human life vary, in each case, the variance is within a limited range. In the case of each, Jesus' last words on the cross remind us in a most existential way, there will come a time when "It is finished." All worldly processes and material come to an end. Planned processes do not simply end. In some cases, they may be finished. The seasons just end. As an agent of free choice, you have a possibility of finishing your life's project...if you took one on....

1

Introduction

In the preface, we noted this is a book written not by clerics or other spiritual leaders but by ordinary folks for ordinary folks. This means that works of great contemporary scholars like Jonathan Kvanig, Linda Zagzebski, Sir John Polkinghorne, Stephen Meyer, Owen Gingerich, and many others will not be referred to since the focus of the book is on meditations for your prayer life. Consequently, the book avoids elaborate arguments and scholarly citations and focuses instead on prompting readers, people such as us, to listen to the feel of God's wisdom and communion with them at those moments.

Principally, this book is a set of guided meditations with only brief reference to three themes: God's Great Gift, God's Great Promise, and God's Plan creating a path for all. Chapters should not be read as chapters in an ordinary book. There is no story to tell. There are no extended explanations. Find an apt meditation in your chapter of choice and try to figure out what, if anything, it might mean for your relation to God and the world of the Divine.

The model of the four seasons is not intended as an exacting limitation on where to begin reading. Each season represents roughly 20 to 25 years of life with God as we remember things. There is no science behind these matters and neither of us is a trained scientific observer nor theologian. One is a university professor who has previously taught courses in business, education, psychology, economics, political science, metaphysics, and philosophy of religion. Unfortunately, such scholarship is of no especially apt utility for writing this type of book. And similarly, the other's experience in the entertainment world is not especially apt for this type of writing, either.

In addition, we did not know one another until we ourselves were transiting from the fall to the winter of life. What we weave together about the themes of Great Promise, Great Gift, Great Plan, and meditative prayer is not wholly of one fabric. Our respective enculturation from the far north to the far south of the United States through nearly all four of the seasons has been vastly different. Despite these geographic and cultural differences, our grasp on the role of living in the embrace of God's Great Promise, and our experience of these three themes is surprisingly uniform. Hence, the uniformity we share with the reader reveals a uniformity of religious conviction that should not be taken lightly.

A glimpse at the guidelines the four seasons model prompted in us

Spring. This ranges from birth to 20 - 25 years of age. Psychologists note this span covers different developmental stages in many ways. Pre-school is dominated by role-modeling. Elementary age is dominated by establishing personhood. Puberty is dominated by quests for popularity and dealing with existential angst. And at 18 – 25 the brain is finishing the wiring of the higher intellective capacities of the brain especially the prefrontal and frontal lobes. By 25, people might become as smart as they previously thought they were.

Summer: Notice there is overlap among each of the adjacent seasons. Summer following spring extends, depending on the individual, from 20 – 25 to 40 - 50. Summer is a time when full adulthood and a sense of social responsibilities become palpably evident in the lives of most individuals. Many people's take on the summer of life involves possibilities for gain, a bit of recklessness in many cases, and new responsibilities, especially should one choose to have children. It may be overwhelming that so many people depend on summerites and expect that summerites know what they are talking about when they are in the summer of life. And, too, often summerites find they generously overestimate what they know or can manage only to have the random vicissitudes of life force upon them new demands for modesty. Recognition of how much yet needs to be learned is unavoidable for any

3

thoughtful summerite. Even in prayer life, something summerites have been accustomed to for more than a decade, summerites often find, again, that they are taking themselves too seriously given their limited experience.

Fall: This ranges from 40 - 50 – 60 - 75. Any children are nearly grown and fallites begin to witness the approaching winter of other's lives as well as their eventual passing. In one's professional undertakings, the peak of one's career can be seen in outline ahead. Illnesses affecting oneself, spouses, and friends are becoming common. One feels more vulnerable and wants assurances that one's religious convictions are right-minded. Sophisticated thinkers begin considering what the project of their respective lives amounts to as they approach the point wherein the time to say "It is finished" is pressing.

Winter: From sixty onwards the realness of becoming the "old people," death, moments of physical suffering ahead all become unavoidable even for those still holding on at the peak of a professional life. Frantic embracing all that sounds good about God and heaven abound in imaginative speculation among many winterites. One of us heard a dying cancer patient ask a longtime friend and pastor "Is it true?" The pastor responded, "I will meet you at the East Gate in a few years." The pastor later recalls his anxiety of what to say in response to the dying patient's question. Of course, the aged pastor admits he knows little about what is beyond and, of course, he knows nothing at all about gates of any kind. Nor, the pastor admits, does he know whether or not the two would ever see one another again. The pastor knew only that his friend was no more than an hour or so from death and needed to hear reassurance that the best of the New Testament poem Revelation could be counted on as true. In such moments of existential angst, what should one be told? To the dying, isn't the Sinner's Prayer and conviction in hand, the assurance the dying person needs when on the brink of death and, hopefully, full communion with the Lord?

The pastor's response was an exercise of the pastor's free will and employed reflecting years of theological learning. In such witnessing situations, the concept of what counts as reasonable becomes palpable. He did right and, as he understood things, he did as Jesus would.

As the example of the pastor's decision above shows, the decisions of winterites can often carry immense consequence for self and others. Of course, all of life is serious business, but, for winterites, there are few diversions that can reasonably distract from obligations that are immediate and inevitable. The winter is the encore, the last act for each in this world. When you visit someone in hospice care or go to a funeral, see if you do not notice a difference between the winterites present and those present who are still in the summer or even fall of life. The seasons of life are bound to affect our prayerful sensibilities.

Why the Chapters?

As noted above the format of collecting the meditations under the four seasons of the year is a matter of reader convenience. Inasmuch as the model was selected reflecting nearly 150 years of our combined thinking of God and all matters religious, each chapter begins with a few paragraphs of text opining on the season of life depicted in the title chapter. Those few paragraphs can be ignored by the reader since the healing heart of this book is not to instruct but to put into the reader's hands a few directions for meditation. Our job is to invite the reader into meaningful prayer. We are not in a position to tell anyone how they should believe.

All readers can read for themselves the same writers we refer to along the way as well as read the Bible. And, of course, the Bible is best read rather than be interpreted to a person personally unfamiliar with its contents. Consequently, rather than pontificate, we hope to induce silence and peace into the reader's mind. We are inviting readers to pray and to receive the wisdom of Lord Jesus and the whispering of God the Father.

Our collective experience leads us to conclude that prayer makes divinely sanctioned possibilities more vivid to the mind. Having already traveled most of three seasons before even meeting one another, our marrying reinforced our spiritual journey as individuals and now as a new social unit that has never existed: namely, *our marriage*.

We do not see God as a puppet master. Essentially, as God said to Noah, this creation is now under your stewardship. I will never again flood the world. I will not be running the show from behind the scenes. Take heart however; I will never abandon you. My creation is here for you to exercise My Great Gift to you: namely, free will. If you choose to mistreat creation, one another, or Me that is a tax that must be risked for you to genuinely have the opportunity to leave your fingerprints on My creation as agents of free will. It is up to you to bless My creation as I have blessed you.

Yes, *God is in charge* but *His choice* in making persons images of Himself is to create a wonder-inspiring world containing all that free-willed humans bring to it. Allowing humans this singularly unique role in creation led God to mandate quantum uncertainty, genetic blending, weather variance, chance, and randomness at every level of creation. God supervenes upon a potentially mundane world the elements of chance and randomness that make the world marvelous, moving beyond tiresome predictability.

The Biblical reference of a plan for "you" is probably best understood as addressed to all believers. Each person is that "you" God is addressing. If God had a plan for each individual, that would run against the **Great Gift of free will.** Humans would only be free to do specific actions and wrong to do anything else. Under such circumstances, free will vanishes in any way meaningful. Destiny would be nothing more than subordination to an algorithm. This is a poor substitute for the free will God genuinely gives.

Consider afresh the plan "God has for you." In the Bible, when that statement is said, it is addressed to no one person. Rather, it is addressed collectively to a group. The group extends beyond those assembled at the time to all who have lived since. THE PLAN is a plan for all persons to learn from his or her individual journey, how to live in the heavenly community destined ahead. THE PLAN creates a wide path for the journey ahead. The GREAT GIFT makes it possible for a person to choose to leave the path altogether at any time throughout the individual's history. Of course, leaving the path forsakes the opportunity of purposively progressing forward to a heavenly reward.

Participation in the heavenly community is a righteous destiny for all, is it not? It is!

But aligning with God's Great Plan and its fulfillment in a heavenly destiny is not a destiny all *must* choose.

To matter at all, free will must mean humans can make choices again and again in the face of many contingencies. Some choices are good, some bad, some indifferent, and nearly all unexpectedly consequential.

Being made in God's image means individual free will *can be used* prudently, leading to apt choices along a broad path all can follow eventuating in participation in divine community. The path is open to all and compels no one. Again, as the apostle James warns, "Faith without good works is dead." Choices abound and actions matter throughout life. A single profession of faith expressed in a magical sentence doesn't cover your bets forever. You must do your best to stay on the path of righteousness.

There are other paths people can choose to follow. For example, the Bible makes it explicitly clear that Satan, too, has a plan for all. Satan's path, as C.S. Lewis and other commentators remind readers, leads away from participation in divine community. These competing paths are also broad, and they, too, accommodate many: namely, those who want an alternative to God's divinely planned path. None of these paths are narrow such that a computer-like intelligence could algorithmically earn eternal reward. The path of God's Plan must be embraced righteously and with resilient conviction despite falls along the way.

There are times of unavoidable bewilderment for those making their way along **God's Great Plan (Path)** for all. But in the midst of every bewilderment, God extends the reassurance of **The Great Promise.** The Great Promise is that He will **never abandon any one person**. But keep in mind, that it is in the nature of a gift, that the beneficiary can always reject it. Free will means persons can reject The Great Promise.

Satan's path is but a few steps away from the furthest edges of the broad path God's Plan makes for all. These alternative paths may run close to one another at times, but they never intersect. Lived experience shows, nonetheless, that it is all too easy to jump from one path to the other. Humans are never banished from God's Path. Think of the parable of the prodigal son. But it is up to the prodigal to make the decision to return while still on his or her worldly journey.

Advancing age introduces new challenges in the lives of winterites. To meet the challenges, the most potent strategy is as it is through all seasons of life: find a quiet space, pray deeply, and listen for the *feel* of God's words. Notice how far you have traveled from the early spring of youth. The distance you have traveled is something to discuss with God in prayer. Question, seek further insight. Don't simply dictate know-it-all interpretations that promise worldly wants. Wants should change throughout the seasons as one approaches finishing one's project of ascending to heavenly community.

Winterites embracing the **Great Promise** and accepting the responsibilities of **God's Great Gift** should celebrate and ponder their current location on the path of the **Great Plan**. No matter what, there will be further bewilderment ahead. But through prayer, trust, and hope is God's promise preparing believers for enduring each new bewilderment with one's soul left unmolested.

Many of the meditations written below were written as we pondered the loss of our parents in addition to good friends such as John, Chuck, Mary Ann, Tom, Norm, Bart, and so many others. These winterites represent a broad range of people we knew and loved, and each has passed. We want to see every one of them in the afterlife…but will we?

Can we offer more insight?

Each author brings something different to the table. Yet if you seek further counsel and you want to talk about the celebratory importance of each meditation in day-to-day life, you are best recommended to chat with the author who loves sociability and hymns of praise, Mrs. Wagner. Together the authors build and repair one another's resources to continue one another's project to the end. Perhaps either this book or Mrs. Wagner herself may help the reader find further wisdom by developing a prayer life.

How Shall We Pray?

The apostles asked Jesus to teach them how to pray. In response, Jesus used words sparingly as He introduced the world to the "Our Father."

Prayer is done best when simple and focused. Avoid distraction. Aim for heart, mind, and soul to become one in divine communion with the Lord. This is prayer. Such prayer is not a matter of alerting God to something He already knows. It is not expressing what you really want. Prayer is about soliciting God's help in understanding what the person praying *should* want.

You pray because you need awareness of your ongoing communion with God.

We know of nothing of Jesus' prayer to God the Father in Gethsemane other than that He asked the Father to take away this cup. His petition was not granted.

Presumably, much else was said between the two. Jesus was in prayer for so long that when He took a break and came to ask the apostles to join Him, they were all asleep. So He went back and continued to pray on His own.

Surely there were few if any words needed between God the Son and God the Father. The two were in the most intimate of communion throughout the silence of Gethsemane. Is there any more paradigmatic example of silent prayer?

The meditations in this book are motivated by the example of Christ in Gethsemane. Think about it. Christ's whole life and, not just the "our Father," is a prayer. The prayer experience of Gethsemane suggests prayer is most robust when delivered in silence. Peace of mind, heart, and soul glide a person towards communion with God the Father.

What matters in prayer is your commitment to find silence of spirit. Trust in the Lord to bring you peace of mind. Trust in His authority to address your inquiry, praise, lament, petition, or confession. In each case, listen. Bring your soul to *feel* the whispering God. Always recall Jesus saying, "My peace I give to you. My peace I leave with you."

Jesus was making no promise at this moment; He was stating a fact! He meant at that moment of communion (the actual event of these words was at the Last Supper) that you and He celebrate unadulterated commitment, tenderness, and love. It is there; pause and feel it.

Using the Chapters

It is probably not a good idea to read more than two or three meditations at a time. As noted above, we believe God whispers. He does not yell. He does not shout. To hear the *feel of God's whispers*, you must be alone with God. Focused on Him alone as He focuses on you. This reciprocal focus is what the great twentieth-century Rabbi Martin Buber referred to when he wrote about addressing God always as one's "Thou," letting all else fade into background. You matter to God and to you God is all that matters during those precious moments of divine communion. (Again, "My peace I give you. My peace I leave you.")

The Covid pandemic was a catalyst for bringing together our thinking leading to some of the meditations that follow. A meditative prayer is not an instruction. It is an invitation you make to the ever-present God to advance your understanding of things you find difficult to grasp.

We walked daily during lock down. In the quiet surrounds, we found a way to express our love towards one another was to talk about our journey together towards God. These conversations were subsequently renewed many a night as we lay in bed in the dark, seeking divine light. Once during this time, one of us had a false alarm about cancer. Following the doctor's expressed suspicion and direction for further tests, we drove to an empty church. In the silence we held one another and we each prayed...in silence. We went home that evening stronger than when we went into church. Each of us felt more resilient about what was ahead. We felt more together than most any other time. God and prayer made it happen.

The substance of the rest of the book is meditations. Do not let the chapter headings or the chapter introductions bias what you expect to find in any of the meditations that follow. Pick each meditation as you need it. Do not rush things. Savor the feel of your efforts at communion with God.

Meditations are not to be read all at once. Pick one, read it. Think about other ways it might be read. Think about ways the meditation may mislead your thinking about the divine. Remember these meditations are written by people just like you. They are not written by God. We do our best to honor God with our limited and well-meaning mortal spirit. We hope God sanctions these meditative expressions of spirit. In any case, the potency of meditative prayer is not in saying certain words but in embracing the authority and love of God directed towards you at the moment.

When you feel confident you have a new angle on your relationship with God, Jesus, or the Holy Spirit, LATCH ON TO THAT MOMENT! This is time for you to study and listen at length and intently to the Divine. You want to keep this moment forever.

Do not expect to hear a voice. It is unlikely you will. Do not keep a running conversation going in your mind *about* the meditation. If you do, you will not *feel* God's whispering to you. You will find instead only echoes of your own desires. Be quiet and listen for anything further coming from Him and not you.

The function of this book is to bring you, the reader, in with us as co-authors seeking communion with the Lord. Your diligent reflection, your choice of meditations, your self-discipline to do no more than two or three meditations at a time are what create the understanding you will achieve as you work with what you find in the following. This is what makes you co-author of all meaning to follow.

When you listen intently and are blessed enough to feel God's whisper, there will be no doubt you have made an advance in understanding. Words at best produce only knowledge. God whispers in feelings. When you are patient, the resonating feeling of God's whispers will be felt in your heart and mind together. The one clear promise God made to all is that He will never abandon so much as one of us. You may not feel Him following a given period of prayer but to be sure, He is there. He is with you and He is in you.

2

SPRING

Creation and Gifts?

God volunteered to pay a tax. He did that for us. He had to do that if He was to make persons in His image. (We use the word persons always to refer to embodied humans. There were humans before Adam and Eve, but they were not soul-fully embodied.) The tax God willingly pays is the consequence of giving humans free will. Importantly, it is free will alone that makes persons in God's image.

To give persons free will, God had to give up being a puppeteer of all creation. For free will to matter, God had to build CHANCE and randomness into creation as Anglican priest and high energy physicist Sir John Polkinghorne explains. Similarly, physicist and lay Torah scholar Gerald Schroeder proposes that God initiated free will when He embodied Adam and Eve with souls. Before Adam and Eve, Schroeder opines, the hominids that had evolved were like other primates and the animals of creation in general. Chance and randomness did not even matter until humans became God's embodied persons. Embodiment is the act of building free will into His

17

creation. How important is free will to God's plan of creation?

God makes an issue of the role of free will in persons again and again in scripture. For example, long after embodying Adam and Eve with souls, God reaffirmed to Noah that persons are meant to be both free–willed AND stewards of God's creation. In this sense, Adam and Eve represent the moment when God's creation became conscious of itself. Physicists John Archibald Wheeler and Saul Weinberg each ponder the significance of this moment when the world (to you readers and the authors, read as: creation) became conscious of itself. God had to create chance and randomness from the very beginning to accommodate His eventual introduction of soul–filled persons.

Self-conscious, free-willed beings can make bad things happen. In addition, for free will and stewardship to matter, God had to build chance and randomness into nature from quantum uncertainty on up. The consequence of building chance into the fabric of creation means that bad things will also happen BY CHANCE. This is doctrinal Bible. God is certainly in charge, but he makes it clear he is done exercising sustained control over all.

Accommodating God's Great Gift to embodied persons is God's Great Promise. God's Great Promise is never to abandon those created in his image. The difference between other hominids and persons of free will began with Adam and Eve.

The gift of free will is very costly. Only God could select an evolved primate and endow them with soul/free will to create persons in His own image. As blessed beneficiaries, our best recognition of God's Great Gift is to FREELY surrender all to commune with and understand God's will for us now, tomorrow, and for the rest of EACH of our lives. We offer to God surrender of our gift of free will and thereby show we are committed to communion with Him in every way.

As with any beloved, the lover always wants to know more about the beloved. Indifference is what follows in the absence of sincere commitment to know more about a beloved. If you love God, then you want to know Him more fully. Consequently, you need to talk with Him, ask questions, and propose speculations and, most of all, listen and feel.

Each meditation below gives you a chance to dwell on one perplexity about your spiritual place at this moment and to share it quietly with God Himself. The answer you are looking for may already be within reach of your personal understanding. When you ask God with no intermediary and patiently wait for Him to whisper, you will learn more each time about what you need to know.

Culture Matters But it is Not All That Matters

Yale psychologist Paul Bloom's research shows that long before there can be any effects of enculturation, young children and even infants, show a sense of sympathy towards one another. Where did this come from? Why is it manifest seemingly before any conversation is present in the life of newborns?

Surely subsequent enculturation adds to or detracts from the speculations of childhood. But as Harvard psychiatrist Robert Coles noted years ago, following investigations with pre-teen children around the world, three questions seem to be endemic in the minds of all regardless of cultural influence. The three questions Coles found all young springites asking: where did we come from? Where do people go after death? How should we treat one another?

Something big seems to be afoot. Existentialists might have cynically denied anything beyond cultural traditions. But Coles' work suggests universally, people intuitively think there is more. Believers want to know what there could be. Non-believers say all is for naught. Both cannot be right. Is there a God? Does God want to share destiny with me?

Why?

As in all chapters that follow, find a meditation and dwell on it patiently with no pressing demands for answer. See where things take you over time. The time that matters is God's time, not yours. Do not press God for an ASAP response. Commit to at least thirty minutes to bring your mind back again and again to the meditation. When you leave your private rendezvous with God, *feel* for His response. It will not be an essay nor a social media meme. Rather, most often answers come as a feel of some oddly new understanding. Bless your journey ahead, and God will bless it as well.

Psychologist Lawrence Kohlberg and biologist Jean Piaget each believed people developed morally from self-centeredness and through stages advanced towards more other-regardingness. However, recent research by psychologists Allison Gopnik at the University of California - Berkeley and Paul Bloom at Yale, shows something very different. In the earliest spring of spingites' years, they seem very sympathetic towards the well-being of others. To the extent that things change as spring wears on, then look to culture.

Very young springites rely on parents and other surrounding adults for the truth of all things religious and metaphysical. In teenage years, springites bring more and more into doubt. Think about it. Regardless of your season, what is a doubt you have about your destiny after death?

Culture is not all that matters, but culture matters. Throughout human life, and especially in the late spring, culture shapes the contours of springites' sense of reality.

The Great Plan calls us to master our free will in service to God and others. At the age of thirteen, one of us witnessed the following. While accompanying a cleric who was a medical doctor and another adult, a university professor, the three of us went to a colony of African Americans living atop a mountain just outside of Hayesville, North Carolina. The cleric was giving free medical care to the people of the colony. The thirteen-year-old was cooking hot dogs for the children.

A half a dozen cars and pickup trucks filled with armed and hooded Ku Klux Klansmen came to the colony that afternoon. They told the three of us to cease bringing food and medical care to the residents of the colony. They also said, anticipating many university sociologists today, that we had no right to come to the South and disrupt their culture. We should go back to where we come from and mind our own business in our own culture. Our ways were simply not welcome in their culture. This was in the summer of 1960.

The Klansmen told us if we were not off the mountain by sundown, we would never leave the mountain alive. To make their point, they grabbed the thirteen-year-old and threw him to the ground. The Klan spokesman then told the two adults that if they care little for their own lives "they should care for the kid's life." The three Christians did not leave until ten o'clock that evening.

Fortunately, there was no ambush. The next day, the thirteen-year-old youngster, full of false courage in the bright sunlight of the new day, asked the priest, "What can we do to get those rascals!" The priest told the boy: "Pray for them as you pray for the people we were there to help. The Lord calls us to service."

The Bible is a miracle

To serve the community of believers, the Bible must be more than a history book. Deciding whether Jonah was swallowed by a whale or a fish trivializes scriptural message. Whether or not the Jonah story is true is no more important than asking if Jesus' story of the Good Samaritan is true. What is important is that these passages have a message true for the souls of all believers throughout the ages.

Consider this: once when Jesus was asleep on Peter's fishing boat, a fierce storm enveloped the boat, alarming all the apostles. Jesus remained asleep. Frightened, the apostles woke him and pleaded for his help. What is the message here not just for the apostles then and there but for every believer even now? The story is not especially interesting as history. There can be many storms and people make it through them, and sometimes they do not. Why does this historical anecdote matter?

It matters because it illustrates God is with us always. Jesus was there to be awakened. They weren't alone. No one abandoned them. Afterwards, they realized God had not abandoned them and all was all right. Jesus was said to have calmed the winds but that was after the lesson was

23

presumably learned by the apostles. Things like storms happen. But rest as Jesus rested. All were together all along – for better or worse.

Many books and even more sermons have been devoted to elucidating the meaning of the "Our Father," the prayer Jesus taught the disciples to say. More often than not, much time is spent on the first two sentences and then on the last two sentences: "Lead us not unto temptation but deliver us from evil. Amen." Little more than a few statements are made to sum the prayer. Does this not leave much to consider? What more is there to understand? For example, does the phrase our "daily bread" refer to physical sustenance alone or to our spiritual nourishment as well? We have nothing more to add to all the speculative writings surrounding this pivotal prayer. Smart people have said a lot, we add nothing by echoing anyone else's words.

In ancient China, there was much talk of a path towards one's destiny with one's ancestors. The heart of the path was found in the directive to "Attend to the roots." In today's world, many would imagine the "roots" lying in the younger generation yet to grow into adulthood. This is not what the ancient Chinese thought. Nor is it what today's Christian should think. Growth depends on nourishment. Nourishment depends on developing root systems sufficient for survival in harsh times. A community's roots are found in the wisdom of elders. So exegesis of the "Our Father" is properly best left, by us at least, to many other authoritative traditions.

But in thinking about the question "How should we pray?" prompts thought as well about "How should we act?" Should not the answers to both these questions fit together?

An acronym popular several decades ago was "WWJD?" (What Would Jesus Do?) By asking that question at arm's length from temptation, a person takes the first step away from evil. Praying and acting well fit together and so WWJD serves as a heuristic blending together as did Jesus, life itself. Life should be lived as a prayer.

Below are some meditations to prompt your courage and increase trust in your own intellectual depth. A loving God is sure to bless and honor your sincerest efforts to commune more fully with Him.

Meditations

Pray for the hooded bullies! How could the Lord want us to pray for and even serve people like that?

 Think about it. Then, think about Jesus dying on the cross. Whom did Jesus die for? Was He being selective and only dying for the good and decent?

 How often do you sincerely ponder the WWJD question in the face of temptation especially alluring to you?

 The quest to be "hip" overlooks the need for robust roots that are deep and broad. Lord, might I read the Bible for the miraculous wisdom it holds. The miracle of the Bible is that it has for each person a timely message for any challenge one might face at any time in history or cultural context. The Bible and often those who have most longingly studied it over decades have much to offer. Help me forego being "hip." Help me find personal direction in the story of Jesus' life and in all the resources of Biblical text.

There are many types of prayer. All good though some types of self-focused pleading do not measure up to genuine prayer. Authentic prayer is genuine effort to reach out and ensure THY WILL BE DONE.

Prayerful intensity is reflected in loss of a sense of self and finding instead a place of communion with God. Imagine focusing on a single leaf in exclusion to all other leaves and all other distractions. Listen while focused and humbly thank God for that moment of his presence in your life. In retrospect, you will recall that all human senses of even the leaf itself disappear and you are alone save for your felt communion with God. God! You will hear nothing, but you will feel his smile.

God promises he will never abandon us. But part and parcel of his Great Gift to us, free will, is that he allows us to abandon him at any time. Pray without ceasing. Learn you are never abandoned. Pray without ceasing. You will see his footprints behind showing that he is carrying you. He may not fix your challenge of the moment any more than he took his son down from the cross. But despite the human lament, "My God, my God, why has thou forsaken me?" he never abandoned His son nor will He abandon you.

 Remember after Christ's lament, when He died, He said "It is finished." Whom do you think He was talking to? Who do you think he was communicating with throughout it all?

 God the father never abandons those who choose to align with his will. How do you, personally, align with God's will?

 Nothing is more comfortable than loving and being loved. God can love as no other. Quietly luxuriate now in the comfort of your embrace of God and His embrace of you.

 Maybe the "Our Father" isn't meant to begin with a plural pronoun. Maybe the prayer is meant to be you and God the Father. Just the two of you in direct communication. Jesus sometimes prayed to God directly. Intimate prayers about the here and now. Father and son and no other. Think of Gethsemane. Think of some prayers on the cross. At other times, Jesus did pray for us-- plural pronoun--but addressed to the singular pronoun referring to God the Father alone. Give it a try now: "My Father...."

Think of one of your hands. That hand is all that exists…until you feel Christ's hand embracing your hand lovingly. At any moment of unease remember feeling his hand caressing yours, his strength undergirding your strength, his peace replacing your unease.

Think of a moment in your childhood that made you very happy. Share that moment with God. Think about how Jesus made that moment so special for you then and now.

What have you offered God today? It is one thing to be full of wants. It is quite another to love God enough to give to Him. You have much to give. Start with any discomfort you feel and extend it outward to Him. He will accept it as your gift to Him.

The Roman emperor Marcus Aurelius observed Jesus would much rather that we imitate Him rather than flatter Him. Do you imitate Him or flatter Him?

Understand Jesus' life as itself a lived prayer. Pray now thinking about the above in the quiet company of the Lord as your guide.

The rain always reminds me of God saying you are safe and welcome inside My world.

Storms and rain are a celebration of God's power and presence. Find the lightning, storms, and rain within you. Then realize that is God's power within you.

Fishing. To the Christian and avid fisherman, it should never go unnoticed that the fish is an early symbol of Christianity. Perhaps the fish icon is because of the two large fish dinners provided to followers. Perhaps the fish icon is because of Jesus' affiliation with the apostles, many of whom were fishermen. In any case, the fish is a sign for things Christian. A sign is always a sign of, or for, something. The Christian contemplating the sign of the fish needs to look more deeply into the depths of his find. Looking deeply enough it is sure to become transparent that the most important catch ever is the embrace of Jesus, God the Father, and a heavenly vision.

Have you any reason to smile today? If not, ask God. He will clue you in. Have you had a chance to thank God for anything yet today?

This is not time for you to assert a personal wish as knowledge. This is time to find a quiet church (any denomination will do), a cemetery, or a place of solitude in nature and ask God not about *your* destiny but about the nature of your *doubt*. What is it you lack if doubt is absent? What is it you have learned that makes doubt reasonable to share with God?

 In the quiet, listen for the feel of God's whisper. This may be your first opportunity to learn more deeply what the Great Promise means to you. Do not try to interrogate God, a practice so natural to early knowing efforts. Now is the time to simply listen. Listen to what God shares. He knows what you are prepared to handle for the time being. You do not. When you do this, you will also experience the importance of humility in authentic prayer. Be patient and be sure to thank God for whatever He shares.

 When the Lord is my shepherd, I shall not want for anything but the courage to follow Him.

 The "Footprints in the Sand" prayer reminds us of when things get rough, we may look for evidence of God walking with us. We look for the accompanying pair of footprints in the sand. Finding no footprints or other obvious evidence of God walking with us we may panic. What about the Great Promise? Where is God now? Has God abandoned us?

He hasn't.

When there is only one set of footprints you can bet it is because that is when He is carrying us.

 If God had a plan to impose on each of us that would run against the Great Gift of free will. Free will would become nothing more than a horrific measure of a person's acquiescence to an algorithm enforced by great reward or punishment. Such would be a poor substitute for the Great Gift of free will we are actually given. The Great Plan He says He has for all is to learn from an earthly journey how to live in the heavenly community ahead. Are you learning?

 Being made in His image means our free will can be used in service to God and others or be cast aside for other transient and earthly diversions. The choice is ours, always ours. This Great Gift of free will means that God has to build chance into the world. In a world of unanticipated good and evil, what we choose aligns us generally with the heavenly community ahead or not. As Jesus Himself said, the souls going to hell fall faster than the leaves falling from trees in the fall. For free will to matter must mean that humans can align or refuse to align with God in the face of many contingencies. What are your thoughts about Jesus' claim that souls are falling to hell as fast as leaves fall from the trees toward the end of autumn?

3

SUMMER

Becoming Embodied Persons: Soul-fulness

After Cain killed Abel, God told the people to stand down and that He would take care of what needed to be addressed. After the flood, God tells Noah he will never again intervene in such fashion. In each case, God re-asserts the Great Gift of Free Will. He tells Noah He has given embodied humans free will to be stewards of His creation. He then directs Noah and his descendants to take responsibility for stewardship of God's physical creation. Moments such as these could be simply statements God knows are factual or they might be, as some believe, promises! Perhaps both.

Why would God bother making promises to elements of His own creation?

How often does God promise things?

How many promises is God responsible for keeping?

These are matters of considerable debate among theologians and the believing community in general. Whatever the right outcome of these debates one thing seems assured. God made one GREAT PROMISE, gave one GREAT GIFT, and laid out one GREAT PLAN to His people. Surely every believer acknowledges the reality of all three.

1. The Great Gift: God gave us free will and a creation that allows humans to leave their fingerprints on His evolving creation.

2. The Great Promise: God promised to never abandon any descendant of Adam and Eve. God promised He had a plan for His people. The plan lays out a broad path for people to follow for heavenly communion with God and others who preceded. God made the path broad enough that, with chance and randomness considered and willful errors on our part at times, all embodied persons can eventually follow the broad and varied path God made possible.

3. The Great Plan: The Bible is more than a GPS of God's planned, broad path. The Bible is itself a miracle. It is a miracle as great in stature as any referred to in the Bible. Do not just agree with the words "The Bible is a miracle because it is the inspired word of God." Think about it! What does really mean to say the Bible, not just its causal origin, is itself a miracle?

Hint: The Bible can speak poignantly to each person over the millennia in times of unique and personal crisis. Across time and place, the believer in whatever condition can look to the Bible and discover: "That passage applies to me here and now!"

Teach Us to Pray

Consider an example from one of the Gospels. When the apostles asked Jesus how to pray, He taught them the "Our Father." What was clear scripturally but not apparent to the apostles - AT THAT MOMENT, was that Jesus' entire life was a prayer!

Ask "What would Jesus do?" each moment in your life and you understand Jesus' life was and IS a prayer elevating believers' spirits even today. The Bible resonates with that message throughout. From Job to the Crucifixion of Christ, the Bible has a message for you pertinent to each crisis of your life.

Again, for example, on a boat in the midst of a turbulent storm, the apostles panicked. Like passengers in an out-of-control airliner, the apostles thought all was over, and yet Jesus quietly slept. When the apostles awakened Him, He admonished them for their panic. He was not sending the message that all was in God's control so not to worry. Instead, He was saying that whatever happens, you are not alone, and God is with you. God will never abandon you. Commit to that, and you will understand what it means to pray. Jesus showed the apostles: Crisis? Yes! Have I abandoned you? No.

The subsequent calming of the sea might not have been part of the lesson but instead a mere addendum. The powerful message that Jesus had to teach was simple: I will never abandon you.

35

The miracle of the Bible and the secret to prayer are part of the same fabric: God promises to never abandon you - that is faith. You can abandon Him, alas the dangerous side of His Great Gift to you namely, free will. His Great Plan gives you a path to follow that helps you avoid the tragedy of those that choose to abandon God.

In Kings, the reader is told; "…do not turn left, do not turn right." God's path is broad enough to accommodate human idiosyncrasies. It allows flexibility. But to turn at right angles to left or right leads off the path and to the abandonment of God.

At one time or another, most people probably fret about just who it is they are praying to…if anyone at all. This is a reasonable inquiry and has prompted many including one of the present authors to publish an article on the "Hidden God" query in *Crisis Magazine*. Paul Moser and others have written entire books on the Hidden God issue in the past twenty years and in the *Journal of the Evangelical Philosophical Society* there are a number of articles addressing this concern.

Even in the Foxhole: Two Stories, Two Heroes

As Harvard psychiatrist Robert Coles found, very young children around the world contemplate God, creation, and eternal destiny. These questions arise again in well-worn fashion in the summer of life for many if even for a limited time. Or so it seems to us.

Most atheists we have met are angry about the very idea of God. Think of the intensely fierce attacks on religion by determinist Richard Dawkins. In his book, *Beyond Love Trauma* (2018), Paul Wagner concludes that hate and love are so intense and personal that they exist as close emotional approximations of one another. Indifference is the opposite of hate. It seems to us that those who hate God and identify as atheists may not in the end be true atheists. They are too engaged in the denial of God to count as genuine non-believers. Between the two of us, we count only one person we know personally who might count as a true atheist. This person was genuinely indifferent to the idea of God. No hate. No agnostic tolerance. Just dispassionate about God or any discussion thereof. Never did she express enthusiasm for her position. Just indifferent denial of the meaningfulness of any discussion of the divine.

In the summer of life, regardless of one's own conviction, each person is sure to come across those who deny and perhaps claim to hate God and believers. What to make of such people?

Will traumatic challenge convert them to religious belief? Doubtful.

Consider just two dramatic examples that led to very different results. Both deal with soldiers who won medals for bravery during the Vietnam War.

In the first case, a reasonable believer from rural Missouri was a Sea Bee on a recognizance assignment with his platoon and a half dozen additional specialists. The unit was on a small hill two miles beyond the perimeter of an airfield the Seabees were constructing. They were dug in. Their fox holes surrounded the top of a hill where the radio technician and senior officer managed operations. At midnight, the platoon was attacked by overwhelming numbers. After a time, the call went out to retreat to the top of the hill to the radio. The fellow telling the story explained that the call to move to the hilltop is a last desperate strategy for those who are alive and ambulatory.

When the sun began rising, the Viet Cong aborted their attack on the few remaining survivors and disappeared into the jungle. By this time, there were only four American survivors. Two were ambulatory. There was no officer, not even an experienced sergeant, nearby, and the radio had been destroyed. What to do?

One of the soldiers walked through two miles of enemy-controlled territory to the American base to get help while the other ambulatory soldier stayed behind with the wounded. Upon reaching the base, the lone soldier had to lead a company of soldiers back to the site of the battle and bring in the helicopter to airlift the wounded. Once back on base, all four were hospitalized. The one who trekked the jungle to secure rescue says he lay down for a nap. He wasn't seriously injured. He awoke a few minutes later only to discover he had slept non–stop for three days.

When asked if he killed anyone in hand-to-hand combat, he grew annoyed and said that was a stupid question. (He had.) When asked if he remembered any faces, he remarked on the naivety of the question. You kill to stay alive, and you kill again and again. There are no faces--only the actions of an enemy trying to slaughter you.

Recall that the attack began at midnight? Remember, too, it lasted until daybreak. Five hours of kill or be killed. The two ambulatory soldiers were each awarded the Silver Star and, of course, Purple Hearts.

The soldier telling the story referred to his Silver Star as a joke. There was no bravery on his part. Just a desire to live and a willingness to fight to make that happen. The Silver Star signals nothing other than luck. He lived, most of the others with him did not, but their fight and death may have helped save his life. It is all just luck.

When asked about God, he became short. He has no belief in God any longer. He saw no evidence of God. He saw only hate, desperation, anger, and luck. He was lucky. End of story.

When asked about the old saying "There are no atheists in foxholes in the midst of battle." He said, "Ridiculous!" He claims he did not think of God even once. He admitted among those who died probably some did and others did not. In the end, it was just luck determining who went home and who did not.

Contrast this story with another Vietnam soldier who won a bronze star. This soldier carries a picture of his four best buddies, all of whom died in combat. He survived the moment they all died. He reports hearing a crisp low voice, presumably God, telling him to "leave now!" At that very moment, he FELT he was securely embraced in God's security, and he found himself surrounded by beautiful flesh-like colors. He left the foxhole. Later a mortar round landed in the foxhole killing all. The soldier believes God spoke to him that day. Did God speak directly to him? Does it matter whether there was a voice or not? What matters is whether he listened and felt truth in the message God was communicating to him. God intervened. But He did not intervene in response to prayer. God simply intervened (and in this case ironically enough, the message was to get out of the foxhole!). Had God tried to communicate this message to the others in the foxhole? Did they just fail to listen? Does it matter how God chooses to communicate? In your mind, are the colors as poignant to the story as the voice? How so? Is it words, sights, or *feeling* that sums the message element?

What is the difference between the two warriors' episodes?

Until we reach heaven ourselves, none of us can say much for sure about the events above. Episodes such as these and many in far fewer exotic circumstances of divorce, illness, financial crisis, and more happen to many readers. Things do not always turn out as we might hope regardless of prayer. And sometimes things seem to turn out well in the absence of prayer. So what should the reader think?

THE GREAT PROMISE is that God will never abandon us and prayer affirms for us the presence of God and the meaningfulness of prayerful communion with God when it is most needed. He promised to never abandon us. And just as He never abandoned His son (though as the human side of Jesus lamented, it sure felt like being abandoned despite Jesus talking to God directly at the moment of His lament). God has promised to never abandon us.

Each soldier was brave. Neither soldier was ever abandoned by God. Neither were the soldiers who died abandoned by God. God is there but He does not push himself on us. Perhaps the one soldier never felt God because he never looked or listened. Perhaps the other soldier was favored because he listened. Did the first hero take God for granted and so remained unaware of His presence? Did the second soldier experience the presence of God because he trusted in the potency of The Great Promise?

One soldier described above thought God does not matter. The other thought God is all that matters. Most importantly, perhaps, is remembering Gethsemane. Jesus implored God the Father to remove this cup and Jesus' petition was denied. Instead of rescue, Jesus was charged to serve. And as the Gospels detail, He served at high personal cost to Self. Other-regarding action shows just how much His life itself is a prayer. Even though He was not getting what He asked for from the Father, Jesus still thought the Father's will mattered most and not the petition Jesus brought to Him in prayer.

Chance

In the summer of life, our new learnings often get beyond our ability to manage them. We learn, for example, that some physicists believe the universe always existed; other physicists believe universes pop into existence from an infinite quantum foam, and some, such as the famed Stephen Hawking, believe that all that exists reduces to a mathematical singularity holding all information needed for physical construction of any and all types. In the summer of life, nearly everyone is going to come into contact with one or more of these theories proffered at the hands of some great minds of physics. These folks are smarter than most people in the world. Surely one or the other of these great minds must be right or nearly right…maybe not….

Start with the idea that before there was something there was nothing. That, of course, will not lead anywhere, so let's acknowledge before there was something. There was the Triune God enduring infinitely into the past as well as into the future. If before the singularity there was only the Triune God, then the Triune God must have created the singularity and all the information it holds! Genesis and the Gospel of John both report that in the beginning was the word, *logos*. Logos is just an ancient word for information. So both the Old and New Testaments concur with much of contemporary cosmology in that in the beginning was the word, the information – filled expression of the Mind of God. Make sense?

So before there was something, there was nothing (beyond God). That also means there was no such thing as chance or randomness at that point either. Chance and randomness came into existence along with all other existents of creation! Why would God build chance and randomness into His creation?

Since God planned that one day there would be embodied (i.e., soulful) persons with free will capacities, the creation must allow for the exercise of free will. The exercise of free will begins with chance shown at the quantum level and up through many dimensions of life. God's plan clearly managed the role of chance and randomness so it did not lead to total disorganization that could not be overcome. The second law of thermodynamics and other fundamental laws of physics God created temper some of the effects of unmitigated chance and randomness well into the indeterminate future.

The quantum world, gases, genetics, and so much else exhibit the randomness God so artfully created. Consequently, humans can have a role (as God explained to Adam and Eve, then to Noah and to others) in stewardship of His creation. In a small way, each person has a capacity and the responsibility to leave his fingerprint somewhere on God's creation. This is how God made embodied persons in "His own image." God is surely in charge at every level. But importantly, He has given substantial *control* of this limited universe to those embodied persons He lovingly promised never to abandon. Keep in mind that God made it adamantly clear that

43

persons are the stewards of His creation. He will always accompany us but will seldom be pulling the strings of puppeteering-like control. Can you handle this?

Meditations

 Does God still matter to you? Even if He is not there delivering goodies for which you implore Him, does He still matter to you? How?

 As Blaise Pascal made reasonably clear, Jesus has given us enough information to make clear it is best to learn and live for the purpose of becoming a resident of heaven than risk such an opportunity of any other less probable alternative.

 Remember Jesus' Life is itself The Great Prayer. Your life, too, is the best prayer you have to offer Him. Once again, call to mind the apostle James, "Faith without good works is dead." A life of prayer is not about merely saying magical words; it is about living a prayerful life! Your prayerful life is comprised of all you say, do, think, wish for, and your stewardship responsibilities God speaks of when sending Noah and his family forward after the flood. What does your life of prayer look like?

Unlike Hollywood, real life cannot be retrieved in an editing room and the bad parts cut out and left on the floor. Summerites begin to understand they have but one life with no "do-overs." What does that life of prayer you are creating look like? Crises and ups and downs of various sorts that cannot be edited do not ruin the prayerful story you are making.

 Drama, comedy, moral indiscretions (Judas' betrayal for example), joy, depression, and more are all a piece of real life. Even Jesus' life of prayer shows He saw and was aware of all these features and more. Your unedited version of what you have lived thus far neither condemns nor qualifies you for reward and punishment. You have yet to finish your masterpiece. The only question at this point is where you go with the story from here. Time to consult with your producer and senior writers, namely God, Jesus, and the saints. What will you make of the rest of your life?

 How much is God's will worth to you? Can you continue honoring and praying to a god who asks so much service of you?

 Do you ever ask God how to best serve Him? Or do you focus on what you might hope to "get and collect" from Him in response to your prayers?

Think now about how you see the function of prayer. Do you pray honoring your vision of the function of prayer?

 Do you ever talk to God about how you should pray to Him? Is there any reason not to ask Him to help you understand prayer better? The apostles thought it proper to ask. Now…you ask.

 What is the fingerprint you hope to leave on God's creation? Before you draw any conclusions, talk to Him about it.

 God whispers. Have you learned that it is in the silence you are most likely to feel His voice clearest?

 To begin, start with Christ on His knees at Gethsemane. The thrust of His prayers was permission to avoid the catastrophic project which would begin shortly and not end until Good Friday afternoon. Surely no one could be better at prayer than Christ himself! So, what is the point of prayer if not to rescue a person or lead to some other good that people can see, here and now?

This very morning is a jewel in the sands of your history; offer it to Jesus.

 Once one of us suffered a very dreadful experience in life through no fault on the victim's part. The victim prayed to God endlessly and believed with fullness of heart. But to no avail. All ended in tragedy. It felt as though God had changed. It did feel as though He abandoned me. But He had not. Nor had I abandoned Him. I fought. I cried. I argued with Him when things turned so tragically bad. He listened. God hadn't abandoned His promise. I came to realize I had things out of whack in my thinking of God and our relationship. He was there for me all along – every minute, every hour, and even every second. He just did not ante up what I wanted. It was then that I realized most fully both his Great Promise and his Great Gift, and He was walking along with me on the Great Planned Path prepared for each and every person willing to align with Him. God blessed me in ways I never understood at the time. He stayed with me until I did come to understand. Are you working with God now, or are you trying to direct His actions as I recklessly did? The first is blessed. The second is not.

What adventure will you and Jesus share today?

 How to pray? Begin by mastering your free will. Align it willfully with what scripture reveals as the prayer that constituted Jesus' life.

 What are wings for? Certainly, in the evolution of life, they have been a potent variant. In art, literature, and even Biblical metaphor, they give WING to human imagination. Wings transport. In our understanding of the Bible, God's will for us requires that our imagination take wing so we can rise above the earthly domain we physically inhabit. Our spirit needs to go to places of mind wherein we can meet God, have Jesus hold our hand, and walk into our own Good Friday: it is a time for contemplating why there is more. Only faith, love, and hope, and the way we live as a result, secures our eternal residence. We are home once we are in the heavenly residence. How will you fit into heavenly community as C.S. Lewis asks?

 Do you think every person has been blessed with at least one family member or dear friend who role-modeled service, freedom from hate, and freedom from slavery to material goods? Is now an opportunity for you to begin such role-modeling for others just as Christ did for all?

There is an enormous difference between virtues and vices. Virtues lead to eternal communion with God. Vices do not. When we think of the divine virtues, HOPE, faith, and charity leap to the forefront of our mind's eye. But other virtues are derivative from the divine. Think of peace, calm, and patience, and there are other derivatives. The virtues in total guide NOT behaviors but rather how we should BE. What would Jesus do? How would Jesus _be_ and what would he _intend_ in each action?

The mind is soulful, never a desert. The rain refreshes. When we feel refreshed, we get outside ourselves. Only when we get outside ourselves can we accept that God is nearby. With the nearness of God in mind, the psychological drought caused by spiritual anguish is seen for what it is: the illusion of a neglectful soul. With God in mind, there are always new and refreshing rains.

What is the bravest thing you have done in life? To what extent were you aware of the Lord's presence in your life then? Looking back on it, how do you now think the Lord was present then?

Think you understand the concept of eternity? Think again. What is an infinite length of time? Two infinities can be the same size, yet one infinity can fit inside some other properly conceived infinity. What do you think about each MEMBER of the Trinity? Any comparisons?

 The moment…this moment is blessed. Explain to yourself how *this moment* is blessed.

 Sometimes the mind needs to be quieted. Sometimes the greatest of intellectual challenges is to put the mind to rest. Fully! No passing thoughts. No reckless declarations about why God creates, the things created are matters of science. Why, he created, and did so as He did and, continues to do so is all a matter of faith -- you don't know that any more than you understand infinity! Struggle with silencing your mind and your psychological impulses. Once you have done that for a few moments, then you will find comfort IN God and that will sustain you far more than a lot of quick answers to things none of us could possibly KNOW! In silence FIND GOD. A recollection of a pleasant moment with Jesus in the past is a blessed distraction for this time. Time to recall that moment now.

The Bible is a miracle. To serve the community of believers, it must be much more than a history book. Deciding whether Jonah was swallowed by a whale or a fish trivializes its scriptural message. Whether or not the Jonah story is true is no more important than asking if Jesus' parable of the Good Samaritan is true. What is important is that each story has a timely message true for each reader in his or her own context throughout time.

God never takes away the gift of free will. You may choose to subject yourself to conditions leading to anxiety. The purpose of prayer is not to make the conditions you choose or suffer to disappear as if by magic. But importantly, as Jesus said at The Last Supper: "My peace I give you. My peace I leave with you." He doesn't take back the gift of free will. Instead, with your prayer in hand, He quiets you and walks with you into the future. He does this every time you welcome Him with prayer. Do you have a personal prayer of welcome that you crafted just for Him?

What do we need to have a robust relationship with God? Love is not enough. How can we possibly reciprocate God's love? Understanding is not enough? How can we reciprocate God's understanding? So what can we do?

Surrender. God's gifts to us are free will and the promise never to abandon us. When we surrender to God, we hold high our free will and offer it in loving submission to God. We do not simply relieve ourselves of the challenge to live a responsible life. When we surrender to God, we set aside any inclination to abandon Him. True surrender is mighty hard. Jesus showed both how hard it is to surrender and, too, that surrendering can be done and done so willfully. Have you ever felt surrendering fully to God?

 Jesus himself was scorned, beaten, and crucified. He prayed in Gethsemane that this not happen. But it did. Are you getting the Biblical message yet?

 You can make amends today or recall some applause, but you cannot change yesterday or luxuriate in an applause indefinitely. Only today is yours! Do, say, or at least think something noble. Pray. Honor God by showing you have learned to serve by praying for others.

 You have valuable time right now to share love with God. Amplify your love of God and His creation by sharing divinely with others. What is your plan for such sharing? Need help? Pray. God will help you with your planning.

 Remember, always, Jesus saying: "MY PEACE I GIVE TO YOU. MY PEACE I LEAVE WITH YOU."

People often ask Jesus to help them carry a burden. Could He count on you to help Him carry His cross to Golgotha? There is much to learn about oneself, is there not?

 Sometimes consider the importance of *giving* in Jesus' name. To be able to give or serve Him is a blessing. Was this not part of the message behind Jesus' parable of the Good Samaritan?

 Keep it simple. Smile for twenty seconds. Empty your mind of *you*. Listen for God's whispers: let go, let God.

 Patience and calmness in the face of adversity is God's gift to us so we might learn from calamity and experience the great blessing throughout life.

 Once, when addressing the College of Cardinals in Rome, the U.S. Supreme Court Justice Anton Scalia pointed out that Jesus could feed thousands at a time. Yet, as Scalia pointed out, Jesus never centered a parable on His feeding the thousands He fed with fish and loaves. Most readers cannot do that. But even if one could, isn't the absence of such a message telling? Instead, Scalia told the cardinals the message of Jesus is more aptly captured in the parable of the Good Samaritan. Each person is charged to serve God's creation as best he can. This parable aligns with God's message to Noah and is heard throughout the Bible. The message is never to force the hand of others to do good when you are not engaged in deliberate sacrificial service yourself. What service can you do for someone today?

Love is a two-way street. When people stop asking one another about their past and their feelings at the moment, it is a sign of indifference. Indifference (not hate) is the opposite of love. So think about it. Does your life with God involve searching communication? Or do you take Him for granted? Has your communication with Him become nothing more than reciting some magical recipes?

How often people quote, "And God gave His only son...." We do not and could not repay God in any way for this gift. But since love is a two-way street, we must ask, "How much, Lord, have I opened myself in love to you?" How much, Lord, do I still attempt to inquire into the life you share with me? In the name of Jesus, I ask that you help me open up more fully to you. Surely, I have more to give, but I need Your whisper directing me how to give more.

If you were to give a sermon about a single word describing your religious meditations and experience, what would that word be?

When you pray deeply and privately, God pitches a spiritual tent around you. Within it, He welcomes you and fills the tent with His love. As Søren Kierkegaard saw, if you can explain that experience to others in words, you have not yet experienced deep prayer and palpable divine love. Focus your attention on the *feel* of such glorious and private love. When once achieved, you will recognize it is an indescribable experience. At that point, you may grasp what Kierkegaard meant when he describes the moment as becoming a "Knight of Faith."

 In the "Our Father" prayer, could the reference to "daily bread" mean spiritual resources as opposed to material goods?

 Take a moment and breathe in the presence of Jesus. It will be sweet. As you feel Him throughout your being, treasure the feel of His presence within you. Treasure the moment free of worldly distraction.

 In the Orthodox Christian churches, followers often use something called the "Jesus prayer" to enter into a transcendental state of deeply meditative prayer. This is the prayer they use: "Lord Jesus Christ, have mercy on me a sinner." (Sometimes they may even abbreviate this further and just repeatedly say the name of Jesus.) You might try this for an hour one day.

 How to pray? Master your free will. Willfully identify what some scriptural passage reveals to you as a moment in Jesus' "life as the ultimate prayer." Contemplate that moment now and its most personal meaning to you.

4

FALL

What Am I doing as I Get Older?

If you are old enough and inclined to read this, then you probably have experienced at least one numbing experience in your life. Imagine the numbing experience of Mary and the apostles after the crucifixion. The apostles were later fearful, lonely, and desperately confused in the upper room. Imagine them recalling Jesus' own words from the cross: "My Lord, my Lord, why hast thou forsaken me?!" What happened to the Great Promise never to be abandoned?

It would be difficult to imagine anything more numbing. Not only Jesus' crucifixion but on the heels of what must have seemed His greatest moments, all was seemingly swept away in hours. They were there to share the good times with Him...did they abandon Him in the bad times? Did God abandon Jesus, Mary, and the apostles all?

Who was Jesus talking to when He said, "It is finished."?

What exactly did the pronoun "it" refer to? What exactly was finished?

If Jesus was referring to His life, then would He not say something more to the point like "My life is over"?

But Jesus did not say that. His last words were about something being finished. Doesn't that usually mean successfully or at least competently completed? But what was completed? He drew His last breath, and it was over.

Note, too, that whatever was finished means that Easter was not the point of it all. Whatever "it" referred to was completed. Easter is an addendum to whatever was finished. So what exactly was finished? What was the point of the project that had finally finished on Good Friday?

Was part of the project that He should be or feel abandonment himself? "My Lord, my Lord, why hast thou abandoned me?"

Was God the Father being merciless?

What was the point? Was it to produce mind-numbing, existential angst in Jesus and His few remaining followers?

Mind-numbing means incapacitating ability to do or imagine purpose. Good Friday seems filled with desperation – nothing more…. Then, something happens. Amid all that happens, there are some peculiar moments that could be quite informative. Jesus cries out, "My Lord, My Lord! Why hast thou forsaken me!" This very cry, however, is addressed to one person and one person only…no one present, no one that is other than God the Father. The cry itself seems to belie Jesus' sense of the presence of God the Father at the very moment of the cry itself. What to make of this?

At the very least, the cry seems to signal that even in what seems total emptiness, when hope and trust are gone, the recognition emerges that you are not all alone. After all, Jesus just addressed God the Father! What follows? Is this moment confirmation of the Great Promise?

The Crucifixion

What was Jesus feeling?

What was "finished," what was "it" that was "finished"?

We cannot tell you nor can any author we have read tell you. But God can whisper meaning that extends beyond the thrust of mere semantic representation. If you want to understand these questions, listen to the *feel* of God's presence meant for you and you alone. It is a treasure--your treasure. A treasure you alone will share forever with God.

Will God share all with you? Unlikely. In part, that is a feature of love. Those we love are those we forever want to learn more about. We love God, and so we go into our own Gethsemane to seek peace and to listen to the feel of God's whispers.

Neuroscientists say that the human brain does not complete wiring the frontal and pre-frontal lobes for executive decision-making until people are between 20-25. Once fully-wired, the season of summer begins. This is followed by the skills of critical evaluation so often evident in the skills and insights of advanced scholars and scientists. They know things. But they are more perplexed than ever by two questions. First, how do we know if what we know is true? Second, since we don't even know what we don't know, wherein should we dig in our heels and demand that others treat our claims as TRUE in every detail? Science believes you are capable of figuring things out beyond what you have been told. We believe religious commitment and honest truth-seeking communication with God can do so as well. What are you figuring out about God?

The focus today is but a single word: PEACE. Clear your mind of each and every thought. Focus on Jesus' gift." My peace I give to you; my peace I leave with you." PEACE, not comfort...not "good feels," PEACE.

In addition to Jesus on the cross, imagine Mary and John at the foot of the cross. Imagine the apostles and other disciples left in emotional agony and overwhelming confusion. Do these mind-numbing events discredit Jesus' claim "My peace I give to you. My peace I leave with you"?

No one can tell you what Jesus felt on Good Friday. In the fall of life, you need to listen. You need to listen as never before. What do you suppose the apostles heard?

What is Good Friday finishing?

You know that Good Friday is the holiest day of the year. But how do you know that? On Good Friday, the promise never to abandon us was complete! On Christmas, God joins with us in a most unexpected but not wholly unimaginable way. We can imagine as we did in the spring of our life what was heralded and celebrated in Bethlehem. On Easter, we celebrate with Jesus His exemplary evidence of redemption. But it was on Good Friday that the Great Promise was fulfilled. How so?

The Great Promise is that He will never abandon us no matter how recklessly we behave. His destiny He shares with us. Despite His closest apostles running from the crucifixion and denying Him, He returned to where they were gathered in the upper room so they could see.

The Great Promise continues, and He was visibly there with them. Remember, The Great Promise is an always promise. God's Great Gift of free will does not oblige us to share destiny despite His commitment to share all with us. God, we love YOU! As a fallite, you have many years of believing some things about God. But now, in this more advanced season of life, talk to God and ask for help in understanding the "it" Jesus was referring to. Why does it seem there was so much apparent abandonment on Good Friday?

At our very loneliest moments, we find the Lord takes our hand. Nothing is said. Nothing needs to be said. God takes our loneliest experience and transforms it into a place of comfort and hope. It is only when we return to the happenstance of temporal reality that the loneliness returns. This loneliness is inevitable. But so, too, is the comfort of the Lord when we let the loneliness of the world sink so deep in our being that we can reach out and feel the reassuring clasp of the Lord's hand on our own. Never alone! Never abandoned.

What might a prayer warrior be? We hear that term a lot. Let's start with what a prayer warrior is not. A prayer warrior is not motivated by hostility towards others nor by material gain. Jesus was a prayer warrior, so start thinking by asking: WWJD in each and every prayer warrior challenge? Is it all about reciting words privately or publicly?

Remember the hermits who shortly after Jesus' death moved to the desert to live sparsely and pray for communion with the Lord. Are they prayer warriors? The martyrs in ancient Rome, Joan of Arc, and missionaries today are not timid but stand quietly like a rock while facing the most hideous forces of aggression--their strength? Prayer. Just prayer? Or prayer in action? Prayer brings prayer warriors into action in communion with God. In contrast to the willful actions of prayer warriors in communion with God, other actions may simply be a product of evolution, luring an animal through the instinct to fight or flight. How do you know when you are acting thinking and speaking as a prayer warrior rather than an instinct-driven animal?

Recall that Jesus replaced the ear of a soldier who had come to arrest Him. What do you suppose was the meaning of that act? This is not a request for you to rehearse some human's interpretation of the event. As a summerite, you should be well along the way to think for yourself. There were no prayers involved, no prayer requests granted by the Lord. Yet nothing Jesus did was meaningless, so what is the meaning here for this exemplar of prayer warriors? In contrast to how you might explain this act from Jesus' perspective, in contrast how might the "get and collect" crowd explain this event? How do you explain this event? What can we learn from this event about being a prayer warrior?

Jesus walked out on water toward where the apostles were aboard their boat. Peter was over-joyed to see Jesus. Peter ran across the top of the water to join Jesus. After a few steps, Peter realized he was doing something thought to be impossible. Plop! He fell into the water. Jesus did not restore Peter to walking on the surface. Instead, Jesus used the incident to teach a lesson. The heart of the lesson is NOT God will whip up a miracle whenever you believe enough. The lesson was that life is about learning and that if we keep trying to learn, Jesus will be there to show you a light in even the depths of darkness. Imagine you were Peter. Think what, if anything, you would have learned from the experience. As always, ask God for help in your thinking right now.

Imagine the courage of Mary. She stood by while her son Jesus was scorned even in the throes of dying. Mary was nearing the end of the summer of her life. What should she be thinking or doing?! Try to imagine her mindset! We can pray for grace hoping we, too, can muster the virtue of her and John when necessary to confirm our love for God. No attention to SELF. All attention to His service. Mary was mortal and yet especially heroic. Truly ask in Jesus' name, for courage and ability to love as Mary showed is possible! Ask this in Jesus' name.

We start off in the spring of life full of innocence. Why doesn't God scoop us up then? We would be such good-natured residents of the Heavenly community. As we get older, our life seems to rot in many ways. Many become cynical. Many become mischievous in the fall of life and beyond and some even become evil, cranky, and ill-tempered. Still others suffer fearfulness and lose trust in others and maybe even in God. Is this the stuff that will populate the citizens of heaven?

Of course, we don't know. But it is a pretty good bet that those decisions to leave the path are compromising their respective individual destinies. What does make a person a candidate for the heavenly community? In a word, could it be WISDOM?

Disparaging experiences are unavoidable. The fullness of adult life encourages turning from disparagement and towards reflection on God and service to Him.

The Last Supper

Jesus knew what lay ahead just hours away. For the sake of the apostles, He stayed calm. He knew his mission was not about Himself but about them and all His followers yet to come. The Last Supper was a historic moment of communion. God on earth in physical embodiment. It was a sacramental moment in Jesus' enormous rescue of us. Here, people such as us and on our behalf joined hands as one family with the Lord of our destiny. Jesus was calm and at peace. He invites you to be calm and at peace now.

Not all prayers are successful. At the University of Pennsylvania, neuroscientist and physician Andrew Newberg studied religious folks attempting deep prayer. They were hooked up to PET scans and left alone in a quiet room. After an hour or so, they would complete their efforts at prayer. Newberg found that when they reported having had "successful" prayer experience, their PET scan, which he then examined, showed evidence of a unique footprint. Even when people of different faiths reported episodes of successful prayer, the unique footprint was evident. When there was no claim of successful prayers, the footprint was not in evidence when Newburg reviewed the scan. Think about the moment of your most successful prayer moment. Learn from that recollected moment.

In the fall of life, you are either at the peak of your social and professional accomplishments or quickly approaching them. So then what? Have these accomplishments led you to or away from God? It is tempting here to say that only you know. But that isn't quite right. God knows.

Meditations

Some friends are dying and more summerites are getting chronic illnesses. You may find yourself thinking of late the old cliches "Getting old ain't for sissies." But what is getting old for? Conversation with God can help you understand. Make an appointment for that conversation with Him now.

Do you want to know about what God knows about your standing with Him? Show Him love. How? By listening to Him rather than the echoes of your own wants and beliefs, you find where you really stand in your relationship to God. To listen to Him and show Him love, you must set aside time, an hour or more of quiet time. Try to cease all worldly thinking. Put pressing obligations aside so you can hear the feel of God's whisper. Maybe there is a foxhole you need to climb out of!

God understands most cannot make a commitment to a monastic practice of daily prayer. Yet you can give God a private audience of your precious time on at least a few occasions each week during this eventful season of life. Are you going to give God an hour or more of your time wholly undistracted by other matters now? Tomorrow, perhaps? Maybe next week? Talk to Him about your plan for a better prayer life.

BE THERE

There is an enormous difference between virtues and vices. Virtues lead to eternal communion with God. Vices do not. When we think of the divine virtues, HOPE, faith, and Charity leap to the forefront of our mind's eye. But other virtues are derivative from the divine. Think of peace, calm, and patience. And of course, there are other derivatives. The virtues in total, guide NOT mere behaviors but rather Christian actions (intended behavior governing Christian actions). How should we BE? Ask yourself always, "What would Jesus do?" How would Jesus *be* in each action, i.e., the virtues evident in His every moment? Choose: virtue or vice…?

Where do you stand in relation to God right now? Is He in the rearview mirror or are your headlights still revealing more to you about Him? Are your notions of Him ahead tempered by the residue of unquestioned tutoring acquired in the spring of your life?

 If you love someone, you always want to know more about the person. Is that where you are with God? Do you want to spend more time in quiet to learn more about Him through the feel of His quiet whispers? Or have you become arrogant thinking "I've got all this down"? Such arrogance brings no one closer to God. Rather, inattention to learning more about God separates you from God's path and lures you onto Satan's path. Be honest. Are you in love with God or growing indifferent…?

 When you stop inquiring deeply into the nature of a beloved, you are destined to look elsewhere for intellectual refreshment, excitement, and fulfillment. Such is true of our human relations as it is with our relation to God. What is it you think you know so well about faith, God, and your destiny? Do you think you've got it all? What don't you know? Your thinking needs to become disquieted, stirred up for fresh beholding of the God whose path you have been following.

New thinking refreshes and keeps the eyes of the soul on God's Planned Path uniting the destiny of all believers. If your inquiry about God is slowing, then, like the sloth, you are easy prey for those walking the other path. Are those you surround yourself with seekers, destroyers, or sloths settling for a less seasoned understanding of God?

 It is time to schedule some special one-on-one meetings with God, alone and away from all distraction. Have you ever considered going on a retreat--a silent retreat?

 Biblical stories are not solely about goodies God intends to still give you or promises of many sorts. Biblical stories, parables, the sermon on the mount and so many other elements of The Word are about sacrifice and service. Through sacrifice and service and no other way, we learn to walk with Jesus evidently in His image. The walk along God's Planned Path leads to comforting others all the while experiencing more divine love and sublime joy.

 Philosopher of religion Josef Pieper believes we can make a place sacred by repeated prayer habits at that place. An empty church, a cemetery, a place in a park you repeatedly visit for the same purpose of prayer: each can be transformed by your actions and intentions into a place of prayer.

Are you feeling lonely…really lonely? By the time you become a *fallite* you should know that God never abandons you. Still, loneliness contaminates each person's life from time to time. Find someone who seems visibly outcast from all that matters to the person. As unobtrusively as possible, present yourself to him or her as a friend. Do not quiz the person or present yourself as a rescuer. You are neither. Simply lend a hand if you can. That is what shows you understand Jesus' parable of the Good Samaritan. Do you?

Most importantly, let the person know you are there specifically for them. Let them know they are not alone because you are there and when you are both there, Jesus is as well. Your sincere commitment to relieve another's loneliness is mirrored in and blessed by the life of Jesus. Action, as opposed to mere behavior, involves intention. Your intention to relieve the lonely of their loneliness is Christ-like. It is faith with good deeds. It mirrors His prayer-filled life. Do you understand that Jesus' life rescued all from unending loneliness?

Patience and calmness in the face of adversity is an instance of God's Great Promise to never abandon you. Struggle with silencing your mind and your psychological impulses. Find comfort in God. His comfort will sustain you far better than a lot of quicky answers to things no one could possibly know about His will. As always, in silence, find God. "Thy will be done."

You are a worthy follower of Christ when you reach out to mute the blaring sound of loneliness in the life of another soul feeling lost and dispirited. Can you be that follower?

Go into an empty church. What do you begin to feel? It is nothing to be analyzed but there is much to be accepted. It is a moment in time, space, mathematical dimension, and you. Take it all in. Do you feel alone? Do you feel lonely? If you do not feel lonely, what is there that while you know you are alone, keeps you from feeling…not entirely alone?

5

WINTER

Is there a Project for You to Finish?

It is winter. The seasons have run their course. When this season in complete what then is in store for you? Is this your end ahead or, in Jesus' last words, "Is IT finished?"

If it is not your *end* then what is it you finish at the end of this season? And how well did you finish?

In any case, there are no further springs, summers, or falls; no more do-overs. Life is like a movie. It is a series of stills which, when spun through, gives the allusion of motion. But to a god's eye view, each scene, no matter how short in duration, is seen clearly and discretely as not in motion at all. A bit of math makes this clear. God is not time limited. Travel backward in time and you will never find a beginning of God. He extends backwards in time infinitely.

Look forward. The Bible reports ahead there is eternity. That means that time extends infinitely and at any point more time can be added. In fact, to be mathematically and theologically correct, an infinite length of time can be added at any point. Similarly, identify any two points. No matter how close they are there are an infinite number of further points between them. This is the meaning of infinitesimal. God, however, can see any and all that exists between any two points. His extension is as infinitely large as it is infinitesimally small. In short, there is nowhere to hide from God. No sparrow falls that He doesn't notice.

The point of this little math lesson is to underscore that when the seasons of your life in this world are finished, God can see all--absolutely all--that existed in your life between your individual origin and your singularly unique finish: What will He see in your life? What would you like Him to see? What have you learned?

There is still time for those reading this to learn a bit more and to do a bit more. Will anything more have merit?

In the 1980s, one of us ran a survey among people over 65. The question was "Assuming your health is adequate, what is the worst thing about getting old?" Nearly 70% of the respondents said...well, let's just wait a moment before telling you the answer.

You are an adult and are probably somewhere past the spring of your life. You have seen some things along the way. Some of you may be in the winter season as are we and as were the respondents to the survey. Surely, an answer so overwhelming repeated by those in the winter season should be easy to predict by most any reader. Do you have your guess locked in?

The answer is but a single word. You can find the word at the bottom of the last page of this chapter.

In the meantime, there are some things we can say about the answer. The winter makes it vividly clear that things – many things – have changed since the spring of life. Winter, unlike any other season, makes it clear that some things cannot be repeated. Things of the past cannot be re-made. They cannot be made better, and they are difficult to make any worse. Winter loads up the traveler with baggage of which there is no way to be relieved. In winter, most find that from time to time they look in the mirror and cannot escape the question: Am I finishing well?

Who's to say if you finished well?

If you finished well or not, what are the consequences? Are there any?

God gave us free will. That meant His plan for us all is that we would use life to some purpose. THAT is His plan - for all. One plan for all with many options available to each for staying on the broadly planned path for all.

God's gift of free will, which He reiterated to Noah and others, is accompanied by the fact that chance will happen. God made clear He is not a puppeteer. The Bible acknowledges even Satan has a plan; a plan much different than God's yet God doesn't thwart Satan's exercise of free will. So who is in control?

That all depends on what one means by in control. God is in charge, and He decided to create a world of random chance so that He could give the Great Gift of free will. The Great Gift is unlikely to be compromised by interjections of control, at least not moment by moment.

Upon seeing the risen Lord, the Bible reports that Peter jumped into the water to swim to Jesus on the shore. Jesus calls out and tells Peter to go back and bring some fish. Jesus did not need to get fish in that way. Nonetheless, Peter obeyed. If Jesus knew what Peter would do, the story would have little point. All would be a mindless exercise, would it not?!

Jesus took a chance and Peter made a choice.

What is the purpose of life!

Just as this book was going to print. Dr. Wagner went into a nearby church following a difficult speed walk he completed all the while suffering sciatica pain. In the church he stumbled hard. He fell and broke several ribs. This led to a lot of time to think and pray. Nearly two weeks later he went back to his injury. He and the Lord kept him moving forward. Still, he wanted to see the place of his incapacitating injury. Paul looked at it and then for some reason he looked up and there on the wall was a picture of Christ falling while carrying his cross. It was difficult not to tear up. He suffered but He kept going. Paul suffered but there right below that picture, the Lord got Paul to his feet, then to the car to drive home, and eventually to the hospital. Jesus knows pain and how to keep going. He blessed Paul with a vision Paul knew the picture of Jesus falling signaled to Paul he had to proceed forward. There is much yet to do for each of us. Just look and see. God is alongside. The Great Promise is unimpeachable. Paul's journey of the last couple of weeks is a new opportunity for prayer wholly in line with Christ's example: never give up, He will never abandon you.

Jesus has taken a chance on each of us. We have a choice to make. We can wander in the turbulent waters of this chancy world OR we can choose to find the placid waters of submission to communion with God and growing towards the community of heaven. The meaning of life? Surely it begins regardless of the season of life, with finding the placid waters of communion with God. Then…choose.

Death. Scary word, isn't it?

No one escapes from it no matter how much we pray. Not even Jesus himself escaped from it. The Incarnate died and was buried. There is no story of a swap from this life into another in the blink of an eye. Dead is dead. But is that all?

It seems that after Jesus died, he did some traveling. Similarly, there are many stories of souls AFTER death that have been active. It appears that after death some things-- things quite beyond any reasonable imagination--happen. Death happened but eventually gave birth to a new life, a new reality.

For Jesus and some others - call them saints if you like, the existence of a new reality beyond is grounds for hope. And here is where the introduction of this chapter finishes. The rest of the work is up to you, the reader.

Jeanene Hanna Wagner & Paul A. Wagner, Ph.D.

Can You Live with God's Creation: Chance Included?

All that exists has happened. As the Bible says, no swallow has fallen that God doesn't know about. Of course, as theologians have noted over the centuries, the tense is past tense. As creator of the universe, God knows the design and large contours of what is ahead but the details are likely to be unknown even to Him. Why is that?

Two reasons. First, if God stands outside of time and is all-powerful, His detractors have a case for claiming either that he is evil or at least complicit in evil. For example, as an all-powerful being standing outside of time, he could see plagues and the Holocaust and Lizzy Borden ahead before the evil they initiated ever happened. For an all-powerful God to do nothing is such circumstances is troubling to theologians and boost to the atheistic arguments of people like Richard Dawkins and Daniel Dennett. But for better or worse, there is nothing in the Bible that dictates that God stands outside of time. The debate will no doubt continue with people arguing time must have existed before God, others that God created time or spacetime others...well, there are many versions upon which people can defend or protest the idea of time and God. The smartest theologians from Augustine's famous argument and onwards will continue. We readily confess any solution is over our heads, but we certainly understand why the debate continues. In any case, as a working hypothesis, we will stipulate tentatively for current purposes that God is timely. This is to say, He cannot be held culpable for any evil caused by humans: for example, Ted Bundy's murders nor nature's unintended evils such as hurricanes, earthquakes, asteroids, and pandemics, nor, as Peter van Inwagen acknowledges, even the fawn struck by lightning in the forest. God is no author of evil. Events that have not yet happened do not exist. God knows all that exists. What doesn't exist simply isn't knowable. It reflects no limitation on God's powers that He doesn't know what isn't knowable any more than when non-believers propose God cannot create an immovable rock that even He cannot move. This jibe of atheists over time proves nothing other than human intellectual entanglement with the semantics we create and employ.

Second, as mentioned elsewhere in this book, it is clear that as Creator of all, God Himself created chance and randomness. Without chance and randomness, there would be no free will i.e., no Great Gift, no evolution, no opportunity for the Great Plan and its path to matter, and so on. His creation of chance and randomness means that beyond general design of the evolving universe, He created a world in which He knows all that exists but nothing of what doesn't exist. That is part of His plan. Beyond general determining design, God cannot know the next swallow to succumb, and this is all a product of God's specific creation. Theologians who tackle this issue of "fore knowledge (knowledge of future details)" often try to resolve the issue by proposing something they call "middle knowledge." (Readers of the *Evangelical Philosophical Society* and the *Proceedings of the American Catholic*

Jeanene Hanna Wagner & Paul A. Wagner, Ph.D.

Philosophical Society have seen an abundance of research devoted to this issue.) Middle knowledge is proposed as referring to the contents of design limiting the future but not entailing details, similar to His absolute knowledge of all that exists (past, present, and general design of the future).

Why is it important to consider all this?

It is important because it helps explain why the Great Promise is so important. An all-loving and powerful God who knew every detail of the future could circumnavigate all evils of any kind for every creature. There would be no need for the Great Promise never to abandon us because it would be impossible for any ill to come our way. Moreover, any seeming ill that did come our way could be explained away as a wonderful good in disguise. For those who want a God who like Santa Claus is always scurrying about to deliver goodies, this is a most appealing proposition. Unfortunately, it runs counter to Biblical themes throughout the Bible. Start with who let the serpent into Eden and what about Job?

Chance and randomness are part of God's Plan. We are not able to tell the reader why. Again, that is more to leave to the theologians. We can however recognize that with chance and randomness in place, the Great Plan for the Path, the Great Promise never to abandon, and the Great Gift of Free Will, and in the image of God all make sense!

Lest the casual reader conclude we are suggesting a limit to God's powers in any way, we are not. Go back to the above and read the analogy to the old saw about God not being able to create an immovable rock and then unable as a consequence unable to move it Himself. Those tricks of sophistry are fine for teaching the nature of paradox abstractly, but they do not apply to the earnest exposition of believers committed to learning more about their connection with the Triune God as is the case in this book about prayer and your individual conversation with God in private prayer.

Limiting knowledge to what can be known is no limit on God. In addition, is it possible that God may still tinker with the world and sometimes in the fashion of a miracle? Surely that is possible. Is it possible God may intervene suggestively in the world? Again, surely, and that comes much closer to our point in this book on personal prayer. When God says to a soldier, "Get out now!" that is a strong assertion. Was it based on knowledge of the future? Or was it based on what He knew about the employment of mortars in the immediate region since God knows everything there is to know i.e., everything that exists? No mortal can claim to know the answer to such a question. But the soldier knows what he was told and, interestingly, God did not force him to leave. In such dangerous situations, God, who never abandons His people, left the soldier's free will intact and would have stayed with the soldier even if he never left the foxhole.

The authors of this book can attest to what we take to be miraculous moments in each of our lives. The story of how we came to marry is filled with far more coincidences than mere chance would seem to allow. Of course, nearly every happily married couple has a tendency to imagine their coming together was more than coincidence. Their union was more they say than mere coincidence. Maybe so. Certainly, we are not in any position to speculate about such. Still, we feel quite certain that, unlike most unions, ours truly was something that seems to reflect Godly intervention. Can we prove that to a skeptical reader? Of course not. Can we feel comfortable sharing our conviction about such with God? We can. And we have. Our story is very complicated and brought together near strangers and clerical intervention and many other extraordinary factors. All to whom we reveal our story cannot help but gasp a silent "Wow." Believer or not, the story is one of a kind, almost exotic. We mention our own story here only to share with the reader that, personally, we each do believe firmly in miracles and divine intervention.

We talk, share, and celebrate these moments wherein we reflect upon our marriage and what seems to us to be God's role in it all. Yet despite such conviction on both our parts, we are not so bold nor arrogant to tell the world we KNOW we were the beneficiaries of select and special divine intervention. While we truly believe we were privileged, especially by God, we cannot defend the position in accord with technical and scientific protocols of public truth identification. Besides, God will tell those that pray intensely and in silence with Him just what they need for their lives. Our personal experience will not make nor break the communion that exists between any believer in communion with the Triune God.

Truth is a representation that maps onto the world without error. As such, truth is an ideal people reach for. But truth is an ideal only God can grasp as unimpeachable knowledge. As mortals, our ambitions are to reach for truth but settle for knowledge only of God's creation and reported word through the Gospels and in prayer.

Knowledge is representation that maps onto the world without EVIDENT error. Think about it. There are many reasons Jesus used so many parables to teach us the Word of God. One reason was that there was never any intention to deliver to us information in algorithmic form. Certainly, we could follow boldly stated algorithms. But there is far more to walking in accordance with God's Plan than to marching along a determinate trail. The Path God's plan sets forth is broadly constructed, so each may leave something of his or her fingerprint on the creation along the way. We are here to learn from failures and successes both. God stays with us, in either case, should we choose to learn from both and continue to lean on Him as needed for further insight. What doesn't exist is unknowable. But as soon as something comes into existence, God knows of it and so we can rely on Him always to help us each navigate the unexpected. No person needs to fall away from the broad path God planned for you. But we can always choose to abandon Him and His path. Such is His love and respect for we bearers of the Great Promise. Soul-fulness, culminating in the ability to abandon the One who never abandons us is an unimaginable beneficence. Honor it always.

"Once saved always saved," denies God's Great Gift and minimizes the value of His Promise. Being saved means living as one saved. The Great Plan creates a path broad enough to accommodate our many idiosyncrasies. The Path of the Great Plan is broad enough that we can always find our way back to the path. Living as one saved means your choice of keeping God with you always. Living as one saved means your choice to continue communicating with Him through prayer. Living as one saved means living with the responsibility given to each of us to be in some way stewards of His creation. The older one gets and the more experience one amasses, especially in the practice of prayerful communication with God, means asking always how we might better serve His creation; it means asking how we might better acknowledge His Promise, honor His Gift, and His saving within the context of His Great Plan.

So now is the time to get better and more frequent with one's prayers. As Donald Rumsfeld once said, "We don't even know what we don't know." That is true for each of us now and in our anticipations of what lies ahead. But what does exist now and that we know of are the Great Promise, The Great Gift, and the Great Plan that will take us to eternal community in God's everlasting community. What more do you need to learn while you still have a chance to be better at communion with God in prayer and then to serve Him now as you will likely do one day in Heaven?

You Managing You

Remember the Johnny Cash refrain, "You got to walk that lonesome valley. You got to walk it by yourself. Ain't nobody else can walk it for you. You got to walk it by yourself." Cash was a devoted Christian when he wrote that verse and he got it right. You have to walk that broad path laid out for us in God's plan alone. Of course, you will have lovers, family, and friends along the way from time to time, but it is your journey. And, yes, the Great Promise is that the Lord will never abandon you, so He is there alongside. But remember, too, the Great Gift, free will. He is alongside for support, but you and you alone must walk the line and complete the journey. Pray to feel His closeness and friendship, but it is not His job to walk the line for you now. He already rescued you long ago.

The most foundational and distinguishing property of human nature, characterizing people even before faith and love is hope. Hope opens the door to faith and love. When embracing all three, the human spirit flourishes. Hope is the singularly unique insight towards a new reality of faith and love beyond, myth and self-interest. Hope is the theme of the 23rd Psalm. Hope brings rest, faith leads us through the Valley of the Shadow of Death, and love anoints us and leads to communion with God forever. All is God's creation, including random eruptions of chance. The

Psalm says, there is a Valley of the Shadow of Death. Fear is natural in the Valley.

There is good reason to fear in the uncertain world of randomness, chance, and even evil. The Psalm does not guarantee any absence of things to fear! Rather the Psalm acknowledges the fearful reality of the Valley and even the threat of other people who are one's enemies. The Psalm calls not for vanquishing enemies or leveling the valley. Instead, it calls for the Great Promise that God will never abandon us. "Thy rod and thy staff, they comfort me." So, with the Great Promise repeated so often throughout the Bible, it is to be expected that people will reasonably fear.

Suffering

It exacts a high cost from those who suffer. Pray that with the high tuition you pay with your own suffering you learn all you can from it. Jesus suffered for you, but He did not do your suffering for you. Suffering with God at your side is the holy grail of new understanding. Prepare for new understanding through the blessing of suffering that is surely ahead. This moment, this precious moment, tell God how you feel blessed.

You can abandon God. Alas, this is the dangerous side of his Great Gift to you: namely, your free will. The miracle of the Bible is that God promises never to abandon you. The Bible is there to help each person keep his or her faith moment by moment.

God built chance and randomness into the world. Consequently, things will go awry with even your best and most responsible planning. What happens then? What should happen then? Think of how often that happened to Nehemiah as he was trying to follow God's bidding to rebuild the city! The chance mishaps were not of God's planning! But Nehemiah understood it was only with God's help that the new unplanned-for challenges could be surmounted.

As with Nehemiah, so God told Noah, you must deal with random challenges. Perhaps retreat to your own upper room and re-group as did the Apostles. As with the apostles, God will be there for you. Quietly listen for the feel of His whispers. Recall his Great Promise to always walk with you. "Always" is a very big word. God can be trusted to mean what He promised forever and to its full extent. Right now, figure out how God is keeping his Great Promise to you at this moment.

God is not a Mr. Fix it as some seem insistent on believing in the spring of life. There may be moments in one's senior years when a person feels abandoned at times as did even Jesus on the cross. Maybe a divorce, a job firing, or a new chronic disease puts an end to a promising and comfortable routine. But God was there, and it was to God the Father that Jesus personally addressed the plea, "My Lord, my Lord, why hast thou abandoned me." Of course, the Lord had not abandoned Jesus. Jesus' own address to God the Father at that time underscores the continued intimacy between the two. And it was personally to God the Father that Jesus uttered his final words victoriously claiming, "It is finished!"

From there, Jesus began new travels and three days later recovered his earthly body. He added some finishing touches to his mission and then returned to the community of heaven and His rightful place alongside God the Father. The final upper room is when all in heaven are together and no longer fear either tragedy or abandonment. Imagine glimpsing your presence in the final upper room.

Infinity is not a number. At least not like other numbers. You cannot count to infinity because there is always more to count. The set of odd natural numbers and the set of natural numbers are the same size, but the odd natural numbers are all inside the set of natural numbers. Does that not make the entailed number set smaller than the number set entailing it? Yet both are said to be infinite in size! Difficult to grasp, eh? So, too, is the idea of heaven difficult to grasp, Infinities and heaven are both concepts difficult to grasp, but that does not mean in either case that there is no meaning to grasp; it reflects only our human inability to do the grasping. For example, think of John's poetic effort dreaming of a walled city with gates and angels carrying swords and such. In the end, we don't even know if the dream was adequately recorded or made up by his scribe Polycarp. These are matters vigorously debated at the Council of Nicaea when questions of what beyond the Gospels should be included as sanctioned scripture. Debates about Revelation's metaphorical potency continue to be debated by theologians today. There are no doubt truths about heaven (as well as infinities) but without extensive description by God such as might be found in the words of Jesus, humans are left to grasping for meaning.

We know Jesus spoke of heaven! But, when He did, Jesus did so sparingly. And even then, He was often deliberately metaphorical in what He said. We do know this about heaven. It will not be boring. It never was and never will be. How long did time extend before the Creation? Infinitely. Since God is all-knowing and all-powerful, He needn't exist in an infinite amount of time, bored. From the moment of creation, we see the divine, before, and after the moment of our universe's creation, extended indefinitely on either side of the creation moment. Jesus Himself reports that He will be "At the Father's right hand" when those who are welcomed choose to join the community.

C.S. Lewis interprets the final judgment as a commitment of indefinite destiny or denial. We do know before the creation it was worth God's time to design the universe's creation. No possibility of boredom there. Had the Trinity lived in boredom, surely Jesus or God Himself would have shared that with humans the creatures He embodied by giving them souls. None, or it would have been mentioned as pivotally important as it is to the destiny Jesus alludes to. We do not know if the goings-on will be as fanciful or archaic as Polycarp's erudition of John's dream. What we do know is that it is worth an infinite length of time to experience the infinity of joy. As Blaise Pascal made reasonably clear, Jesus gave us enough information to make clear it is best to learn and live for the purpose of becoming a resident of heaven than risk any other alternative.

Sometimes not understanding is a good thing. It is much better than misunderstanding. Misunderstanding means a person is just wrong. Not understanding admits to an allure of unexpected possibilities. Surely nothing of the moment can be good! But how do we know?

All we know is that Jesus, like each of us, died. And we know that Jesus told us there is more thereafter. Jesus could have told us, but He did not. Probably because there is no way a mere human at this point could understand it. Jesus told us what we needed to know and kept silent about what we needed not to know and could never understand at this point. Jesus did tell us there is a point. Jesus did tell us there is no last point. We don't understand…and so God gave us hope and conviction in the power and reliability of God's endless love for us. Impossible to understand right now, but there it is draped in the allure of celestial beauty.

CANCEL CULTURE!

Stop the racing mind that so easily spins out of control in the face of our social surrounds. Our only peaceful refuge is found in silence, prayerful silence. In prayer-filled silence, we find our acceptance of God's promise never to abandon realized. In the silence, we hear His whispers.

Extend your silence and try to understand His comfort and the meaning of His whispers to you and you alone at this moment. Realize you are awash in God's blessing--at this very moment! Not tomorrow, not yesterday, but now, this moment.

Sacrifice is an opportunity to get to know God better. The devil is a strong believer in God, but he understands nothing about love, commitment, and sacrifice to the glory of the Lord. What is a sacrifice you might make to share your respect and love for the glory of His work?

Anxiety can be mild or intense, chronic or acute, dominant or controlled. You can live well much of the time regardless of the extent of your anxiety by surrendering to God. Know that Jesus will give you His peace now and will leave it with you as He promised. He will leave His peace with you for the rest of your life and beyond.

And as C.S. Lewis proposed, some who made the journey did not get wisdom. As a result, they do not want to venture into a place they never tried to understand, namely heaven. Heaven was a place these souls soured towards along the way. A long life well-lived sums in wisdom and appreciation for divine communion. A life long or short, which closes its eyes to wisdom, trades free will for endless unsatisfiable wants. Those soured on the idea of heaven abort the journey along God's broad path and settle instead for dizzying despair, abandoning God and they die...they just die....

Sometimes when things are most bleak, these are the times of potential clarity as you stand pleading before God. Sleep well with God at hand.

Church is not a place to run to in order to escape your challenges. Church, the Bible, prayer, and sacraments are all about accepting Jesus' peace and securing its fear-limiting force, time and again.

Fear and worry are not from Satan, but Satan can use them to amplify their potency to separate a person from Jesus and His ever-present peace. Do not run and hide from anxiety and Satan's advances. Church and Jesus are nearby always. They are there to restore the inner core of your spiritual strength. If you doubt their omnipresence, look at the cross and think about what Jesus was role-modeling for you. Toughen up just as Jesus is preparing you.

Now, the answer the winterites gave to the question: What is the worst thing about getting old? Guilt.

Meditations

At our very loneliest moments, we find the Lord has taken our hand. Nothing is said. Nothing needs to be said. Our loneliest is transformed into a place of comfort and hope. It is only when we return to the happenstance of temporal reality that the loneliness returns. This state of loneliness is inevitable. But so too is the comfort of the Lord when we let the loneliness of the world sink so deep in our being that we can reach out and feel the reassuring clasp of the Lord's hand on our own. Never alone! Never abandoned.

No experience is hollow unless we make it so. As Albert Einstein said, "Everything should be made as simple as possible. But NOT more so." To declare an experience hollow is to make it too simple. To pontificate that an experience is beyond earnest evaluation leads to over-simplification. For example, no one knows all that went on in Christ's mind at Gethsemane, but everyone can imagine what such impending tragedy might have felt like to Him. We know

He asked the cup be passed. That is all we know from hours of His praying. Is this meditation on something simple or complex? Think you know about the concept of eternity? Think again.

 Unlike a Hollywood movie, no one can go back and edit scenes from one's earlier life making some better and dispatching some from view altogether. Is the movie you made one you can be proud of or rejoice in even when fully unedited?

 Because you are reading this, it is clear that your winter is not yet over. What can you do now and tomorrow to better serve God?

 What can you do now to finish well? Can you share in the Lord's love now in ways you never before imagined? Is this moment of prayer a unique and extraordinary blessing for you? Explain it to yourself.

 Reasonable and mindful fear is implicitly acknowledged in the 23rd Psalm. Is the 23rd Psalm an ode to trust? What might your answer mean when looked at in-depth?

The apostles retreated in fear and insecurity to the upper room following Jesus' crucifixion. Where is your upper room? Tragedy awaits everyone. Construing the Lord as a comic-like figure who has a plan and goodies galore for you just around the corner may be a fun idea, but it has no place in reality of Judea-Christian scriptural texts. God chased Adam and Eve out of Eden. God condemned nearly all in Sodom and Gomorrah. God can be tough and foreboding. He is not now, nor has He ever been, the adult image of Santa Claus; nor is He an analogue to an ATM machine in which one deposits a prayer to get some goodie. We know of a fellow who tested the Lord by increasing his tithe. As it turns out the fellow did better in business the next year. He concluded his (bribe?) increasing his tithe did the trick just as he believed the Bible told him it would. So he was continuing his increase for another year.... Is this your image of human relationship to the Lord? Now that you are old, you have seen your share of disappointments and prayers that seem to have been ignored. So who is this person you pray to?

Why should you pray at all? Have you known God long enough to know more than just stuff about Him? How well do you know your best friend? Now compare how well you know your best friend with how well you have knowing feelings for God. Think about knowing God. What does it feel like?

How do you suppose God sees you feeling a certain way about Him? How do you suppose He wants you to feel about Him? After the flood, God told Noah, you are now stewards of all this I created. You handle its management. Being made in My image, you have free will. You are charged to use your free will to create a management plan for your surrounds. You must execute your plan respectful of Me and all My creation. Does having such God-given responsibility scare you? What would make the assignment of responsibility less frightening?

 Do you address God intimately in times of seemingly unanswered prayer and despair? See what Jesus did and remember His entire life was a prayer. Make your prayer to God now in what you think, say, and do--serve the Lord as did Jesus.

 What is an infinite length of time? Two infinities can be the same size, yet one can fit inside the other. What do you think about each MEMBER of the trinity? Any comparisons? Sometimes the mind needs to be quieted. Sometimes the greatest of intellectual challenges is to put the mind to rest. Fully! No passing thoughts. No reckless declarations claiming all is a matter of faith. You don't *know* the truth of most of those declarations any more than you understand infinity! Silence your mind and your psychological impulses. Only then you will find comfort IN God. And that will sustain you far more than a lot of quicky answers to things none of us could possibly KNOW! In silence, FIND GOD and your way of aligning with Him.

WHY ME? Do you ever ask that question? How often do you get answers? Never? Or nearly ever? Chances are answers are coming but not in textbook sentences--not even in scripture or in some pastor's sermon. But the answers are coming if only you will listen for the FEEL of them.

We are here to learn. That is why all that happens to us each, happens. No fairness or unfairness about it. Each moment is a tutorial. Are you earnest and ready to learn? Do you sometimes let this unique and treasured moment slip by?

Do you ever just visit with God? Sometimes just sit or kneel and ask for nothing. Just quietly share time with God. He knows you well. And time is the most important asset any person has to share. Share some time with God.

What do we need to have a robust relationship with God? Love is not enough. How can we possibly reciprocate God's love?

 Understanding is not enough. How can we reciprocate God's understanding of us? What can we do? Surrender. Trust; He will take it from there.

 God's great gifts to us are free will and the promise never to abandon us as we travel along His broadly planned path for all. When we surrender to God, we hold high our free will and offer it in loving submission to God. When we surrender to God, we set aside any inclination to abandon Him. Surrender is so hard. Jesus showed us both how hard it is and, too, that it can be done.

 God gave us free will. This gives us a chance to be architects of our future. He stands with us every step of the way as we craft that future. Jesus says: "My peace I give you. My peace I leave with you." He doesn't take over your life. Instead, He walks with you into the future to the very end. Surrendering to God means asking and truly listening to His advice. Surrendering to God does not mean escaping responsibility for your actions. Can you imagine doing a better job in your life than by listening to God?

Again, look at the movie you have made through the seasons of your life. Is it worth watching?

What makes the movie of your life worth watching? What would you now edit out of that life movie? How can you finish the movie to accommodate scenes that are unavoidably part of your story?

How dismaying is it to know there are no options open to you for editing the movie at this point?

Who might find it worth the time to watch the movie of your life? And why would anyone take the time to do so?

How can you make a worthy finish of your life's movie from this point onward?

You are certainly empowered to bring your life to an **un**worthy end. This is because of God's Great Gift of free will. Keep in mind, there are no encores. So your plan for pronouncing "It is finished" as Jesus finished His own project on Good Friday will sum in what?

 What is life for? More particularly, what is your life for?

 It is a dazzling bright sunny day. God is smiling on you. A pleasant moment from the past is a welcome distraction for you. This moment is a jewel in the sands of your history. Can you share this radiance with God right now?

 Demosthenes was said to have hung a heavy sword suspended by a thin line above his throne. His reason for doing so was to remain mindful that this moment could be his last to do good. Ionesco's *Exit the King* is about a king who always intends to do good but only after he gets over an illness plaguing him at the moment. As fate has it, he never quite gets better, so nothing gets done, and…he dies. Which one do you think understands the moment better: Demosthenes or Ionesco's king? How good are you at making this moment divinely purposeful?

Jesus' message was not meant to be a fairy tale pretending that no crisis ever ends in a bad physical outcome if only one believes. Jesus' message is that no matter the threat and no matter the outcome, those who are faithful to God's Great Promise will never be abandoned-- NEVER. Is that enough for you?

 In hospice or palliative care, there is so much new to learn. The tuition is high. But there is no other way to learn what those experiences have to teach you. Death is inevitable, but your learning from it is not inevitable. This is the moment wherein the Holy Grail of understanding is at hand. Are you ready to pay the tuition? God is standing by.

 God wants to visit personally with you today if that is okay with you. Your learned intimacy with God is something only you and He share and can understand. Find His comforting grace shining throughout your person.

 Lord, please rescue me from my own selfishness.

103

Remember the answer to the question about the worse thing about getting old? 70 % of the seniors said GUILT. Why guilt? At this stage of life, there is often little chance to make amends. Lying, cheating, rudeness, theft, violence--so many things caused by you. Of course, it took Christ dying on the cross to make us right with the Father. But even with such divine intervention, it doesn't change the fact that we did those grievous sins that rightfully embarrass and trouble us. So what to do in the time left to us? Live as you should have lived all along. Commit no violations of others' well-being. Find ways to model the Good Samaritan. In short, muster now all the commitment you are capable of, and commit to being the good person you would like to be and to present to the Lord. God forgave your sins. But is there an antidote for your well-earned guilt? Yes! It is ***Commitment to do good!***

6

AND BEYOND....

What is good and do you have to be good?

There is an enormous difference between virtues and vices. Virtues lead to eternal communion with God. Vices do not. When we think of the divine virtues, HOPE, faith, and charity leap to the forefront of our mind's eye. But other virtues are derivative from the divine. Think of peace, calm, and patience. And of course, there are other derivatives. The virtues in total guide NOT behaviors but rather how we should BE. What would Jesus do? How would Jesus *be* in each action?

This chapter starts off with an odd title does it not? And yet it addresses a question people have surely been distracted by over time. The death of Christ to atone for evil, the evil of anyone or all of us sounds cold. The Bible does say "What greater gift could anyone give?" That is how much God loves us. But why did His love have to be shown through the death of His only son?

Is there some kind of divine, moral economy or jurisprudential system of quid pro quo? Where did it come from? Would a forgiving and loving God create such a

107

system? Must a loving and forgiving God be subordinated to such a system? The less-than-serious believers will just ignore such questions and immediately return to a list of wants to be fulfilled. But to more serious believers these questions are inescapable. Sincere believers want to understand more about the God they truly love. True love makes it impossible to escape from reflection on such questions. Without entertaining such questions, what is the substance of belief? Without entertaining such questions, then where does faith enter Christian life?

Below, we will not have answers for you to any of these questions. But we hope the meditations you choose below will bring you into fuller communion with God. Will you understand all? No, but you will understand more just as the apostles did at the Last Supper and during Christ's visitation in the upper room after His crucifixion.

It is highly unlikely that there is an economy of sin and goodness requiring God to pay off the debt for your sin, or that He would be willing to do so by allowing the torture and crucifixion of His only Son. Where is God's love for Jesus in all of this? And if Jesus is also God, where is responsible self-love? Do these questions scare you? Talk to God!

Several times throughout this book, we have proclaimed that to our way of thinking the Bible is a miracle and should never be reduced to a mere history book. We have suggested that Christ's life in its entirety is a Great Prayer. If you want to know how to pray on a grand scale, as always ask: What did Jesus do? Why did Jesus do it? And at this moment in my life, what would Jesus do? This is authentic acknowledgment of the Great Prayer exhibited through Jesus' life.

If Jesus' life is THE Great Prayer, then there is no retribution or quid pro quo economic bargaining at play here. Instead, having given Adam and Eve and their descendants, embodied souls capable of free will, the Lord surely wanted people to have the freedom to do good (but that entails the freedom to do otherwise as well.) God tried to capture Adam and Eve's attention about the importance of freedom to do good. But by ignoring His one command, it became clear that people did not yet have a grasp on how to be in God's image and manage free will.

After the flood, the message seems again to be, "Take notice of what it means to be free to do good." Think of Sodom and Gomorrah. Humans have a difficult time grasping what it means to optimize freedom! Freedom is optimized when humans do good. When we do wrong, are we not acting slavish to baser instinct and in defiance of where love, surrender, and free will would naturally lead? Think of Christ's life as the GREAT PRAYER. Through it, He is showing us that life is a journey wherein should all go well, we learn to be candidates for heavenly citizenship. See what Jesus does. See that it is not done **for** some reward.

Jesus exercises the ultimate in freedom by choosing each time to do good: end of story. The citizens of heaven must surely be those who have a grasp. "What would Jesus do?" With the life of Christ, God role models what being

Jeanene Hanna Wagner & Paul A. Wagner, Ph.D.

in the image of the Creator should look like. Christ's life is instruction.

Science and Religion: Natural Bedfellows

Dr. Story Musgrave was an astronaut who fixed the Hubble telescope while it was in outer space. Dr. Musgrave took nine hours of graduate work in philosophy with Professor Wagner. The night before Musgrave was to launch in the space shuttle to travel to the Hubble, he called Professor Wagner at home. For two hours, they talked about all that might be real. From the subatomic world to the furthest reaches of the universe and the embeddedness of the universe in God or at least in God's plan. Together the astronaut and medical scientist and the professor of philosophy pondered where all things end. Ironically, a few years before, both attended a party at Shuttle Commander Dick Scobee's home. This was a few months before the Challenger catastrophe. Knowing Scobee and the crew's end led to discussion of the "end" all that night before Musgrave's launch. We shared lots of questions and hypotheses. We were open to one another's critical evaluation and speculations. We were not setting science against religion. Why would we?

Instead, we were thinking together to understand more. We did not get answers from one another. What did we get?

We got questions to take to God the next time we each were alone with Him in silence. Did God answer our questions? Was that really the point? Or was the point as we each thought, simply to bring us closer into communion with God by having the conversation with Him and not soliciting answers for some celestial, standardized multiple-choice test.

Is science the enemy of religion? Not a chance. Some of the greatest scientists alive today are religious: Jim Tour in nanoscience, Donald Knuth in computer science, Sir John Polkinghorne and Gerald Schroeder both in physics, Vernon Smith, Nobel Laureate in economics, and many more. Recent research claims that the overwhelming majority of members of the National Academy of Sciences are not believers. On the other hand, two-thirds of Ph.Ds. in the physical sciences generally believe in a spiritual realm of some sort.

Science is a product of our God-given stewardship. It should be respected and honored as such. And regardless of what any scientist might say in favor of or opposed to destiny and the divine, your contact should be based on your experience with the whispering God.

Philosopher William Alston wrote that it is through experience of the divine that we get to know Him. Later reading of scripture is meant to fill in some blanks and to guide each person further as a result. In this guess into the beyond, we offer a trail created by three atheist scientists but whose views, despite their intent, lead suspiciously to favorable conclusions about God and creation.

Before listing the three, here is a note to file away in your thinking. Of the world's three greatest physicists, Aristotle, Newton, and Einstein, Sir Isaac Newton wrote two-thirds more about theology than about either mathematics or physics. He was among many who contemplated math as the language of God's creation. Now here are three atheist scientists in recent history whose work leads us at least to feel heartened in our experience with the whispering God.

The first scientist is Claude Shannon, the father of information theory. The second is Nick Lane who in his recently released book *Transformation*, argues that all that is relevant to life can be reduced further than genetics, further than any material in fact. All can be reduced to information! Does that sound consistent with much of religion?

And then there is physicist Stephen Hawking who reverse-engineered the equations of cosmology reducing all that exists, every particle and every force to a mathematical singularity. This is not a physical singularity. It has no height, no width, and no depth. Yet in this singularity is all the information for all of creation. Oddly, does not the Bible declare in the beginning was "the word (information)." And all that exists came from there. So contemplate Hawking's mathematical singularity chock full of every bit of information ever needed for creation and beyond and what do you come up with? Do not think of this as a proof of God or creation. Rather share with God your thinking about such matters. Your job is not to prove anything. Your job is to converse with God. Let Him lead you into the feel of greater understanding of a world containing natural and supernatural dimensions.

Ask God to guide you in matters of stewardship service, HOPE, faith, charity, and most importantly, perhaps invigorate your trust in Him by listening for His feel.

Just Keep Things Simple

The word of God is in the Gospels. The first great preachers James, Peter, Paul, and others are not the word of God. They wrote sermons. Their words are sincere. At the Council of Nicaea, their sermons, written as letters to congregations, were included after the Gospels as appendices - *epistles* - to counsel followers from time to time just as today's clerics do. But for the word of God, look to the beauty and simplicity of Jesus' words.

Jesus did not speak like a wordy scholar or scientist. He used allegory, metaphor, and analogies that every follower for the rest of human history could focus on and meditate upon. Jesus' voice in the scriptures prompts reflection and focus on God's continuing dialogue with each of us. James said, "Faith without works is dead." Paul suggested you are saved "not by good works but by faith." These are sincere clerics trying to sort things out.

If you are troubled by these differences between the apostle's Epistles, return to the Word of the Lord; it is in the Gospels. Read a few words of Jesus. Then meditate

Jeanene Hanna Wagner & Paul A. Wagner, Ph.D.

upon God's word. In the end, what matters is to be Gospel-driven. Advance your meditation by asking in quiet and alone…What would Jesus do? Jesus taught us to live and pray by mirroring His life. Our effort to mirror His life is the grandest of all prayer efforts.

What is Heaven like?

Of course, we want to know what heaven is like! For any believer, it is a notion impossible to avoid. In the Gospels, Jesus tells all about the wonderful place he has prepared for each resident in heaven. So whatever is in heaven, it must be good. Then again, in Genesis, the reader is told when God finished creation all was good…hmmmm…. And surely, we can imagine more than a few people in history saying about their experience of God's creation: Really…not so much.

So what is the good of heaven? John's dream or at least Polycarp's recording of it as John recounted it to him as the old man's scribe tells of an analogical world full of things folks in the here and now, at the time, could imagine. But that is not the same as telling us what in fact are the contents and processes of the place. Jesus' words about the place He will prepare for eternal residence in heaven for each faithful believer presumably indicates this much. Not only will all in heaven be good, but it will feel good as well. Just what does that mean?

Positive Psychologists such as Mihaly Csikszentmihalyi and Martin Seligman claim that research shows people are

114

happiest when they are outside a sense of self and are challenged. Here might be a clue for you to talk with God about how to learn more about heaven.

Some tricksters talk as if heaven is a place of partying and material grandeur. The writer Rod Stirling wrote a script of the "Twilight Zone" wherein a non-believer went to just such a place after dying. The non-believer was not unlike many professing "believers" who make up what we dub the "get-and-collect" crowd. The "get and collect" crowd are those for whom all good is summed up as the stuff one gets to *get and collect.* Stirling's non-believer in the afterworld gets all he asks for and every activity works out just as he wishes...always. The non-believer gets painfully bored and admits to what he takes to be his personal angel, that he had always been a crook and his death was at the hands of police trying to stop him in his latest crime. He proposes that he probably ought to be reassigned to "down there." He just does not belong up here. His personal "angel" begins laughing sardonically and cackles "Up here?! You are already where you propose you belong." In short, Stirling's hell is exactly what the get-and-collect crowd are hoping for: goodies, nothing but goodies.

What else is there?

A Parent's Moment of Unmatchable happiness

Remember the positive psychologists saying we are most content, most deeply happy when outside ourselves and focused on challenges to benefit others rather than SELF. Could this be true? Is there a Christian message in this?

One of us has no doubt about the single happiest moment in life. A son asked what gift he could get for his first real girlfriend for Christmas. Her family was very wealthy and the pretty, young girl never wanted for anything. As a freshman in college, she had a big new car, clothes, credit cards she never had to give an accounting for and her parents use to take her and my son to Durango to go skiing by way of a leased private jet. When asked what he was thinking about getting this girl for Christmas he said, "There was a pair of running shoes she admired in the mall."

Dad asked, "Have you ever seen the movie "Bridges Over Madison County?" He had not. Dad went on to explain, "This is puppy love you are dealing with. Ideally, you will give her a gift that regardless of what direction your lives may take she will find this gift one day in an attic or garage and remember her first love. I have an idea. Our family ranch was a special place for you two when no one else was around, right? I have a professional artist coming to paint scenes of the ranch. I will have one painted for you to give to her." He said, "Oh Dad, that is your generation. A girl of my generation would never want something like that."

He got her the shoes. And unbeknownst to him, Dad had the painting made. On Christmas morning, she got the shoes and expressed her appreciation, "Thank you." At the end of the morning, the packaged painting was discovered behind the tree and given to her. When she opened it, she seemed to lapse into a catatonic state – no movement, nothing. Eyes down on the painting in her lap.

When she looked up her eyes were filled with tears. She put the painting down and reached out to hug my son right in front of everyone (she was normally quite shy). Holding her and seeing me in the background, he gave me a thumbs-up and a massive smile. That was the single best moment in my life. I was outside myself. I fulfilled a challenge with God's help and blessing. No one could ever give me some stuff to outdo that moment of grace. What's the point here?

If getting outside oneself and accepting challenge is the greatest joy possible, then maybe in heaven, joy will be found in the challenge to serve the Lord more fully than ever dreamed of before. Could it be?

Of course, we don't know. But it does seem plausible, does it not? Certainly, a greater joy than the *get-and-collect crowd* can imagine. You want to know more about heaven. Read Jesus on the matter. Then, as we have said so often before, go in silence to talk to God. Lay out your thoughts to Him and then, mostly, just listen.

What's the "worth" of heaven?

There is no way to know much detail about heaven. Jesus certainly had no intention of bribing followers with the promise of endless goodies. Jesus said He will be there and that He will prepare a place for us. Since Jesus is the ultimate authority on heaven, we can certainly bet on its existence as Pascal proposes in his famed wager with his gambler friend. Beyond the promise of heaven's existence, there is little else to go on. There are implications that there will be much to do and that things will be divinely nice. More than that, no one can really say. Given the broad path traveled to get there and the lessons of Jesus about the Good Samaritan and the beatitudes, presumably commitment to service and great virtue will permeate the lives of all who commune with God for the rest of eternity.

The idea of heaven as merely a place to "get and collect" for one's own well-being is nowhere near the mark. Think what you will bring to serve God and others in heaven. If you are reading this, you are alive. You may not be able to make many amends for past infidelities and such, but no one is excluded from completing the journey on God's grand path save for those whose druthers led them to choose another path instead of one God put before each embodied person.

Meditations

 Starting today, what acts of service will bring you into communion with the others in heaven?

 Who exactly do you intend to be in the minutes, hours, days, weeks, and years ahead before the moment of heavenly judgment presents itself to you? This is the most important decision you will ever make. Are you up to the task?

 What do we need to have a robust relationship with God? Love is not enough. How can we possibly reciprocate God's love? Understanding is not enough. How can we reciprocate God's understanding? What can we do?

Get outside your SELF and **Surrender to Him**!

 God's great gifts to us are free will and the promise never to abandon us. When we surrender to God, we hold high our free will and offer it in loving submission to God. When we surrender to God, we set aside any inclination to abandon him. Surrender is so hard. Jesus showed us both how hard and that it can be done.

 Your winter will come to an end. Your life will end. If there is a new reality beyond, will you get to take part?

 How can one be an active participant in a new reality, a reality that is heavenly?

 The final steps along God's Great Planned and broad path lead to destiny, celebratory...or not.

The rain always reminds me of God saying you are safe and welcome inside His houses of worship as you will be in heaven.

 Role model, the Great Prayer of Jesus' life. Unfold what it means to be in the image of God. Is this worth retrieving a Bible for a little more reflection? Will such thoughts in silence with all attention devoted to the Lord help you ascend in communion with Him?

 In Gethsemane, the rock where Jesus prayed is itself symbolic. Away from others, Jesus went on bended knee. The rock symbolizes unshakeable faith, trust, belief, and love.

121

Epilogue

If we have succeeded, you have found meditations worth spending a lengthy period of time thinking about. Finding more reason to affirm your conviction in the Lord is a sign of love, respect, and willingness to learn. Finding reason to question the meaning of a meditation can be a success. Questioning the well-intentioned accuracy of the meditation can also be a success; anything bringing you closer to feeling the voice of the whispering God is a success. Even disease, new birth, and a host of other events can bring the prepared mind closer to communion with God.

We live in a time when people are washing their hands of religious affiliation. According to the Pew Research Center, nearly 25% of those who identified themselves as members of a church now claim to be a "None." A *"None"* is one who believes in a theistic metaphysic but refuses to affiliate formally with any given church or set of doctrines. Evangelists have been especially hard hit according to Pew Research Center. In 2016, approximately 15 million people identified as Evangelicals of some sort. By 2020, using the same research protocol, only 12 million still identified as Evangelicals.

The reason for these changes is way beyond the scope of this monograph and is best left to scholars, theologians, and social scientists and not to ordinary folks such as us to ferret out. But speaking in our ordinary voices as authors, we are concerned that an apparent drift away from religions is occurring.

People are social creatures and need a church home. Sure, people can pray alone and in silence to God. That indeed is the sole mission of this monograph. Help people pray in silence and *feel* the whisper of His response. Yet most people are typically not like the desert fathers in ancient Egypt (and even they found occasion to meet periodically with other religious hermits for a communion with others equally devout). The life of the hermit of monasticism may be a select calling for a few. But most of us travel along elsewhere on the Great Path.

Religious centers bring people together on a regular basis to remind us that communion with God is to be done both collectively and in private. The authors here leave to those who are scholars to define and explore the various aspects of theology, philosophy of religion, cognitive animation of prayer, and social dynamics of religious practice and affiliation. This monograph is largely a set of prompts for feeling your way thought-fully toward the Lord on your own. Praying relentlessly is not a matter of using a lot of words.

Meditations

 When addressing God one-on-one, the individual's words should be kept to a minimum and verbal contributions made pithy. The rest is to wait and listen for God's whispers. Do not try to anticipate what God will say. Instead, listen, just listen.

 Trust, the whispers will come, at the time, a bit after the prayer session and maybe not until the next day. Do not worry. Trust, the feel of His whispers will come. Trust, He will carry you when you think you can no longer manage on your own. Trust, He will never abandon you. Trust the Great Planned Path has plenty of room even for one stumbling along such as you and the two of us.

 Take some time to converse with God about what a believer's trust in Him should look like, feel like, and develop.

Take your understanding of The Great Plan, The Great Promise, The Great Gift, and then pray. Read the Gospels, and then pray; Read the entire Bible, and then pray. Serve the Lord and others, and then pray. Be responsible in carrying out the stewardship of God's creation as He charged, and then pray. Remember Jesus' parables and the Sermon on the Mount. They are featured jewels of Jesus' teaching. Finally, find the silence and pray.

Authors' Biography

Jeanene Wagner has experience with movie production, acting, modeling, music production, and thoroughbred horse racing. She has also been a Bible Study Group Leader on several occasions throughout life. This she has combined with volunteer work both in Emergency Room Care at a major teaching hospital and in a pregnancy crisis center. She has traveled extensively over three continents. In addition to leading Bible studies for women, she has appeared on several Christian podcasts. And she has traveled to Israel several times and twice was baptized in the Jordan River.

Paul A. Wagner, B.S. Political Science and economics (double major), M.A. (philosophy), M. Ed. (Higher Education Administration), Ph.D. (Philosophy).

Dr. Wagner has always been very active in civic and charitable affairs. Beginning in Columbia, Missouri, he served as Vice Chair of the City's Human Rights Commission. In Houston, Texas, he has served on numerous Board of Directors including the Houston Marathon, Leadership Houston, The Houston Volunteer Center, The Bay Area Symphony Society, Bay Oaks School, and numerous committees in organizations such as the American Cancer Society, the Society for Prevention of Cruelty to Animals, Second Baptist's Pastor Prayer Team, the Linda Lorelle Scholarship Foundation, and the Sparacino Dance Company. He has done consulting in strategic planning and management practice with a number of corporations, hospitals, and universities, such as The Houston Chronicle, M.D. Anderson Hospital Volunteer Division, and the University of San Francisco. He has also held a number of senior-level positions in scholarly organizations. He was named an Outstanding Young Man while in Columbia, Missouri, and has been awarded inclusion in the following since then: Who's Who in America, Who's Who in the World, Who's Who in Education, Who's Who among America's Teachers, to name but a few. He has taught at universities from coast to coast and from the northern Midwest to the South. He has taught from undergraduate to doctoral students. At the university level, he has taught in the following areas: philosophy, psychology, political science, education, cognitive science, economics, "Development of the Sciences," management theory (in MBA program), organizational behavior, and applied ethics in a course for doctoral students in two different doctoral-granting institutions. One course was titled "Ethics, Values and Responsibilities" and the other, "Ethics of Administrative Leadership."

For thirteen years he emceed and was an expert commentator several times each year for public television. In addition to living in Houston for forty years, he also had a small ranch out near Brenham, Texas. He has run over 50,000 miles in his life according to running journals he has kept since he was 28. He has over 160 publications listed on Google Scholar including nine previous books. He is a member of a number of professional organizations including the American Philosophical Association, the Evangelical Philosophical Society, the American Psychological Association, the American Association of Public Administrators, and the Association of Practical and Professional Ethics. Finally, he was a founding member of the Texas State Ethics Commission and the LBJ School of Public Affairs, University of Texas annual Ethics workshop for senior State Officials in the 1990s. To top everything off, he was an altar boy from 11 – 13 years old at St. Barbara's Church in the suburbs of Chicago.

Jeanene Hanna Wagner & Paul A. Wagner, Ph.D.

Suggested Further Readings

A few books mentioned in this book that some readers might enjoy for a more rigorous read of background information:

Any book by C.S. Lewis or Peter Kreeft

Dale Allison, *The Resurrection of Jesus*

William P. Alston, *Perceiving God: The Epistemology of Religious Experience*

Paul Bloom, *The Sweet Spot*

Robert Coles, *The Spiritual Life of Children*

Mihaly Csikszentmihalyi, *Flow: The Psychology of Optimal Experience*

William Lane Craig, *God, and Abstract Objects: The Coherence of Theism: Aseity*

Richard Foster, *Celebration of Discipline*

Scott Hahn, *No Greater Love: A Biblical Walk-Through Christ's Passion*

Peter van Inwagen, *The Problem of Evil*

Søren Kierkegaard, *Fear and Trembling*

Nick Lane, *Transformations*

E. V. R. Kojonen, *The Compatibility of Evolution and Design*

Alfred Mele, *Free: Why Science Hasn't Disproved Free Will*

Stephen Meyer, *Return of the God Hypothesis: Three Scientific Discoveries That Reveal the Mind Behind the Universe*

Thomas V. Morris, *Our Idea of God*

Thomas V. Morris, *Divine and Human Action*

Leonard Mlodinow, Stephen Hawking: *A Memoir of Friendship and Physics*

J. P. Moreland, *The God Question: An Invitation to a Life of Meaning*

Andrew Newberg, *How God Changes Your Brain*

Blaise Pascal, *Pensées*

Christopher Peterson & Martin Seligman, *Character Strength, and Human Virtues*

Sir John Polkinghorne, *Belief in an Age of Science*

William Rowe, *The Evidential Argument from Evil*

Gerald Schroeder, *The Science of God: The Convergence of Scientific and Biblical Wisdom*

Richard Swinburne, *The Resurrection of God Incarnate*

Richard Swinburne, *Was Jesus God?*

Gary Thomas, *Sacred Pathways: Nine Ways to Connect with God*

Paul Wagner, *Beyond Love Trauma (last three chapters and the appendices)*

Jordan Wessling, *Love Divine: A Systematic Study of God's Love for Humanity*

Ben Young, *Doubt*

Ed Young, *Voices of the Heart*

Other books by
Paul A. Wagner, Ph.D.
published by
Third Coast Books, LLC:

Love Trauma, 2016

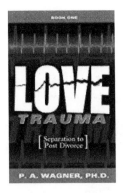

Beyond Love Trauma, 2017

Other articles in both popular and professional journals by Dr. Wagner that may appeal to the reader are as follows:

Wagner, P. (1983). The Idea of a Moral Person, *Journal of Thought,* 7 (1): 35-49.

Wagner, P. (2005). Whispering Truth, *Crisis,* 23 (8). 17-22.

Wagner, P. (2005). The Church of Convenience, *The New Oxford Review,* 72(11) 10-13.

Wagner, P. (2006). Truth and Apologetics, *Crisis* 23, (7/8) 12-14.

Wagner, P, & Benavente-McEnery (2008). Genuine Religious Belief: Is it a Thing of the Past in Public Schools?. *Interchange* 39 (3) 327-350.

Wagner, P. (2021). The Science and Metaphysics of Addiction. *Open Access Journal Psychology and Addiction.*

Wagner, P. (2021). Lives Live on the Edge of Contradiction. *Psychology.* 11 (5), 191-198.

Wagner, P. (2021). What is the Importance of the Abrahamic Avoidance of Naming God: A Platform for International Agreement?, *Cultural and Religious Studies.* 9 (7) 342-347.